RSAC

RETHINKING A LOT

ERAN BEN-JOSEPH

RETHINKING A LOT

THE DESIGN AND CULTURE OF PARKING

THE MIT PRESS
CAMBRIDGE, MASSACHUSETTS
LONDON, ENGLAND

MIT Press books may be purchased at special quantity
discounts for business or sales promotional use. For
information, please email special_sales@mitpress.mit.edu
or write to Special Sales Department, The MIT Press,
55 Hayward Street, Cambridge, MA 02142.

This book was set in PF Din Text Condensed Pro by
The MIT Press. Printed and bound in Canada.

Library of Congress Cataloging-in-Publication Data

Ben-Joseph, Eran.
ReThinking a lot : the design and culture of parking /
Eran Ben-Joseph.
    p. cm.
Includes bibliographical references and index.
ISBN 978-0-262-01733-6 (hardcover : alk. paper)
1. Parking lots. 2. Sociology, Urban. I. Title. II. Title:
Design and culture of parking.
TL175.B46 2012
388.4′74—dc23
2011026441
10 9 8 7 6 5 4 3 2 1

CONTENTS

PREFACE

It was the early 2000s, and I had very big shoes to fill. I was just starting my career at the Massachusetts Institute of Technology (MIT), and part of my teaching obligation included a course titled Site Planning. Site Planning is not just any other course at MIT; it is the oldest continuously taught course in the School of Architecture + Planning. Moreover, since its first offering over 75 years ago, it has been taught by only a handful of instructors, many of whom have turned out to be luminaries of urban design and city planning.

In 1956, a newly tenured professor named Kevin Lynch took what was then seen as a mainstream course in site engineering and turned it into a whole-system approach to planning the built and natural environments. His soon-to-follow book titled *Site Planning*, published in 1962, reflected this unique thinking and is still considered the field's foremost textbook. The text, notes, and resources from the course's collections are comprehensive and include topics such as earthwork and grading, utilities and infrastructure layouts, and the design of access and circulation systems.

One of the common topics covered by the course has been the allocation, siting, and planning of parking lots. Although it is well researched, thoroughly explained, and informatively detailed, one element was missing—there were no documented cases of well-designed surface lots. Over the years, many of my site planning students further pointed out this deficiency by asking: "Are there any good examples of notable, or 'great,' parking lots?" I could barely think of one.

To some extent, this book is a partial attempt to answer this question. In the spirit of Lynch's holistic approach to site planning, I have tried to look at parking lots as more than just utilitarian objects. Can parking have beauty and greatness in the less than obvious traits of aesthetics or form? Can the way people use lots, both planned and spontaneous, be a significant determinant of importance? Are surface parking lots just transient, residual way stations in our built world, or do they hold cultural and historical virtues?

I have been extremely fortunate that these questions have also intrigued others who, in return, have assisted me along the way to finding some answers. First, I owe a great deal to the students who took the site planning classes at MIT, and to those who have worked with me on this project. To Kathleen Ziegenfuss, who wrote her master of city planning thesis on strategies for using parking lots as public spaces: I gratefully acknowledge your intellectual and substantive contributions. To Max Thelander, Trinity Simons, and Rachel Blatt for their research assistance in gathering material and summarizing it in a concise and meaningful way. To Thomas Oles and Jeremy Shaw for collecting and recording intriguing parking lots around the world. To Stephen Kennedy for turning words into evocative graphics and for partaking in a creative interchange of ideas.

At the MIT Press, thanks go to Roger Conover for his encouragement, enthusiasm, and wise advice in converting a rough idea into a book. To Anar Badalov for his patience and for making the editorial process a pleasurable and fruitful experience. To Gillian Beaumont for her insightful editorial suggestions and keen and critical eye. To Margarita Encomienda: my appreciation for your ability to tie it all together in an elegant graphic fashion. To my colleague Alan Berger: thank you for sharing your amazing aerial photography. Outside of MIT, I need to thank the numerous architects, city planners, urban designers, faculty members, and just interested individuals who have answered my inquiries about notable parking lots, and have shared with me a wealth of information and photographs. To Jon Fain and Sam Bass Warner: thank you for your editorial assistance and thoughtful suggestions.

Finally, to my family and especially to you, Holly, for being an inspiration, an intellectual critic, and a constant source of encouragement, love, and support. I could not have done it without you.

A LOT ON MY MIND

On August 20, 2002, the headline of the *Weekly World News* claimed, with bold black letters: "Ancient Parking Lot Found on Mars!" Proving "that alien civilizations DO exist." While most are sure to dismiss the supermarket tabloid for its outlandish cover story based on a paranormal theme, its satirical outlook and reflection on our society cannot be ignored. As the newspaper eloquently explains: "You can learn a lot from a society by their parking lots. . . . Does a violent society create horrific parking, or does horrific parking create a violent society?" We do not have all the answers, the newspaper continues, "perhaps the stories of Martians trying to conquer the Earth are true. They might have simply run out of places to park."

While the Martians may have run out of parking spaces, Earth's supply is steadily growing. In fact, it is estimated that 500 million surface parking spaces exist in the United States alone—a number that increases every day.[1] In some U.S. cities, parking lots cover more than a third of the land area, becoming the single most salient landscape feature of our built environment. While parking space statistics for other parts of the world are not readily available, the sheer number of cars produced in the world can provide some indication. In 2006, for example, it was 49,886,549. In 2009 it was estimated that over 600,000,000 passenger cars were traveling on the streets and roads of the world, and ultimately searching for parking. The search for parking spots will only intensify when one considers that China became the world's largest car market in 2009, when sales soared by nearly 40 percent to 13.5 million units. Yet penetration of the car in China is still lagging, with only 24 vehicles per 1,000 people, compared with 749 vehicles per 1,000 people in the mature markets of the G7 nations.

The question of parking is intensified by the fact that 95 percent of the time cars are immobile.[2] One could plausibly argue that a hybrid Prius and a Hummer have the same environmental impact because both are parked the same amount of time and both occupy the same 9-by-18-foot standard rectangle of paved space. Regrettably, most of us do not spend much time thinking about parking unless we are looking for a space. Yet those paved spaces have vast impact on the design of cities, and the character of our built environment. Large impervious surfaces increase runoff and affect watersheds, while exposed pavements increase the heat island effect of cities. Parking lots are usually considered a necessary evil; unsightly, but essential to the market success of most developments.

The basics of parking lot design have not been significantly rethought since the 1950s. For the most part, parking is regulated by local zoning ordinances. If design is controlled at all, the focus is on size, entry and egress, and occasionally buffering to mitigate visual impact on surrounding businesses or residences. Most parking regulations deal not with the design of the lot, but rather with the minimum number of spaces required for new developments. In most cases, these regulations call for greater and greater amounts of parking set aside for peak use, which is usually applicable only a few days of the year. Still, generally, all standard parking spaces are designed exactly the same, despite the fact that some spaces are used every day, some are used only once or twice a year, and some may never be used at all. In her famous song "Big Yellow Taxi," Joni Mitchell laments: "They paved paradise and put up a parking lot." Although many may indeed be longing for a future where we tear down a parking lot and put up paradise, the reality is that parking and parking lots are here to stay. As long as our preferred form of mobility remains with personal transportation modes, the car (whether powered by fossil fuel, solar, or hydrogen) will continue to dominate our environment, cultural and social life. The question of where we park it and how we design spaces for it remains as essential as questions about the types of car we will use in the future. So situated, the surface parking lot is a landscape ripe for transformation. Extracting more of its value, embracing its cultural importance, and increasing its usefulness are long overdue. The question is: why can't parking lots be modest paradises?

One look at a typical parking lot raises many questions: Can parking lots be designed in a more attractive and aesthetically pleasing way? Can environmental considerations be addressed and adverse effects mitigated? Can parking lots provide more than car storage? Can they be integrated into our built environment—not only as a practical necessity, but also as something elegant and enjoyable? What can we learn from studying usage behavior and manipulation of lots by unlikely users such as kids, food vendors, theater companies, and sport fans? And finally, are there any great parking lots that can inspire alternatives?

0.2
"Ancient Parking Lot Found on Mars." © Weekly World News

0.3
Parking lots are everywhere, and despite their
prevailing dullness and mundane design,
they are an integral part of our culture and social
way of life. As long as our preferred mobility
remains with personal transportation modes,
questions of where we park our cars and how we
design spaces for them will remain essential.
Within this dynamic, the surface parking lot is a
landscape ripe for transformation. Frisco, Texas.
© Alan Berger

0.4
Rockville Town Center, Rockville, Maryland. © Bossi

0.5

Traditional parking lot design, or lack thereof, has created seas of shimmering car hoods, or worse yet, empty, windswept dead spaces, vast expanses of pavement with the occasional island of withered shrubs and stunted trees that provide minimal shade. © B. Tse

0.6

It is estimated that 80 to 90 percent of all U.S. parking demand is provided by surface parking lots. These numbers are not unique to the United States. Parking lots are in great demand worldwide from Asia to Africa to South America. They are considered a necessary evil—ugly, but essential to the success of development. Left: Arras, France; center: Luanda, Angola; right: Tokyo, Japan. Left: © Lode Dom; center: © Angolaone Village Initiative; right: © David Lisbona

ReThinking a Lot addresses these questions by exploring the origins of the surface lot, its impacts on the built environment, and its influence on our culture. Despite their prevailing dullness and mundane design, parking lots are an integral part of our culture and social way of life. They should be treated not as a residual space of our built world, but as an integral part of it. Embracing the lot's utilitarian use, acknowledging its appropriateness, while uncovering ingredients for change, are the goals of this book. The book argues that molding everyday places through simple, generative interventions can transform the way we live and interact with our surroundings. The intent is not to champion the abolition of surface parking lots or to advocate the creation of strict codes and standards that dictate their design, but rather to illustrate their ongoing contemporary effects on our life and their great potential for the future.

The literature of numerous experts covers other important aspects of parking, from parking demands and parking ratios to curbside parking and structured garages. For example, Donald Shoup's excellent book *The High Cost of Free Parking* deals mainly with cities' parking requirements, curb parking management, and parking's economic costs. *Lots of Parking* by John A. Jakle and Keith A. Sculle thoroughly examines parking lots and garages, and the land uses associated with storing automobiles. Mark Childs's *Parking Spaces* is a comparable endeavor to *ReThinking a Lot*. With a combination of design principles and engineering research, it demonstrates and promotes techniques to support an active pedestrian environment, and establishes an alternate setting for vehicles.

ReThinking a Lot does not seek to provide a survey of the diverse forces shaping parking policies, nor to describe the vast engineering and design solutions for accommodating the car. It does not, for example, cover parking garages, their construction or their influence on the built environment. This specific parking typology is well covered in architecture literature. Books such as *The Parking Garage: Design and Evolution of a Modern Urban Form* by Shannon McDonald, and *The Architecture of Parking* by Simon Henley and Sue Barr, deal with the history, influence, and style of garages and specialty buildings designed to house the car.

ReThinking a Lot focuses on the open parcel. It celebrates both the existing and the potential lot. It embraces the surface lot, does not reject it, and strives to raise awareness of its importance. In the process it also gives attention to the lot's history, its potential for design innovation, future change and modification, and environmental and cultural promise.

Each of this book's three parts consists of highly illustrated short sections. Part 1, "A Lot in Common," discusses the pertinent issues associated with surface parking lots and their urban morphology. It highlights planning and design approaches to the parking lot, along with commentary on cultural and artistic attitudes and uses, and focuses attention on parking lots' environmental impacts, aesthetics, and social influences. Part 1 sets the background and establishes the argument for rethinking the lot.

Part 2, "Lots of Time," reviews the history of the surface parking lot: how it was formed, where it was developed, who was responsible for it, and how it has evolved. It covers the historical policy and design shift from curb or street parking to off-street lots, and examines the establishment of regulations for parking lot capacity and design geometries. Finally, it covers the urban morphology shift from the city core parking phenomena of the early twentieth century to the suburban and rural parking lots associated with the strip and the mall.

Part 3, "Lots of Excellence," focuses on a paradigm shift. It points to the conditions that have ultimately led to change in the design and planning of spaces for cars. It illustrates initiatives and innovations developed in response to environmental concerns, and explains the technical know-how, integration of ecological goals, and flexible standards critical to the creation of better, well-suited and multipurpose parking spaces. "Lots of Excellence" also showcases a few examples of great lots from around the world. Each example includes a description of the project, an explanation of its uniqueness, and a visual presentation of its key innovations.

—

No doubt parking lots will continue to exert their influence on how we perceive and shape the built form of our global landscape. Their utilitarian purpose provides fertile ground for innovation and experimentation. While the parking lot's ultimate outlook will inevitably evolve in response to the future interaction and use of the automobile, its physical form and usage could guide the way we shape physical space. It is the aim of this book to help unmask the potential of these common places, and pave a new way for their design.

0.7

In some U.S. cities, parking lots cover more than a third of the land area, becoming the single most salient landscape feature. Lots for regional malls can take up to sixty acres. Houston, Texas. © Alan Berger

0.8

Young Guineans study under the dim parking lot lights at G'bessi Airport in Conakry, Guinea. Only about a fifth of Guinea's 10 million people have access to electricity, and even those who do experience frequent power outages. With few families able to afford generators, students discovered that the airport parking lot is one of the few places where the lights never go out. © YAP Photo/Rebecca Blackwell

0.9

Bluegrass parking lot pickers. Parking lots are more than places for car storage. They are also the setting for many planned and spontaneous activities, from farmers' markets to improvised basketball games to tailgating at sporting events. © Bobby Smith

0.10

Planners, designers, developers, and the public rarely pay attention to the design of parking lots. Most parking regulations deal not with the design of the lot, but rather with the minimum number of spaces required for new developments. © Corbis

0.11

Carpark—Members Only by artist Matej Andraž Vogrinčič has over 15,000 toy cars glued on a vertical brick wall adjacent to an actual parking lot in Adelaide, Australia. © Rebecca Thomas

1

A LOT IN COMMON

1.1
The parking lot is society's modern-day common. © Dan Pieniak

1.2
Parking lots—banal in appearance, and ubiquitous. Do they hold the potential for the greatest transformation as a single-category land use in our environment? Laguna Niguel, California. © Alan Berger

Parking, like driving, has been a fundamental part our everyday life since the invention of the automobile. In the beginning, the few automobiles on the roads parked alongside horses and wagons at the curbside. As the "horseless chariots" took over cities and towns, the need for storing and parking them had to be accommodated outside of the street space. To ease this ever-growing need, municipalities and private entrepreneurs started to offer off-street parking.

As this part of the book shows, off-street parking solutions may have alleviated the initial congestion caused by haphazard parking, but it has not improved the quality of our cities and public spaces. While we all recognize that parking lots are an important part of our transportation network, too often little consideration is given to how they are designed and their impact upon the land. Parking lots are also a central part of our social and cultural life. They influence the way we drive, the destinations we choose, and the way we behave while looking for a parking space. They can breed feelings of both danger and dependency. They also provide a certain inherent flexibility that stimulates spontaneous (and sometimes planned) public activities such as hosting festivals and markets, or a place to celebrate the car and sport culture.

The cultural geographer Paul Groth asserts that the parking space is one of the most important and most underappreciated aspects of the present-day urban environment. He explains: "The ancient Egyptians organized their life and their gods in reference to the life-giving Nile. Colonial New Englanders organized their village life around the axis mundi of the meetinghouse, the place that manifested their connection to the cosmos. Although it happens just below the level of awareness, the parking space probably generates the most significant sense of personal and social place in the cosmos for today's urban Americans; it is their major axis mundi."[1]

MEDIOCRITY

I am tempted to dwell on the importance of the parking lot. I enjoy it as
an austere but beautiful and exciting aspect of the landscape. I find it easy
to compare it with such traditional vernacular spaces as the common:
both are undifferentiated in form, empty, with no significant topographical
features to determine use, both easily accessible and essential to our
daily existence. But on another level, the parking lot symbolizes a closer,
more immediate relationship between various elements in our society:
consumer and producer, public and private, the street and the dwelling.
J. B. JACKSON[2]

Throughout his illustrious career, the landscape writer John Brinckerhoff Jackson argued for the "Love of Everyday Places." Unlike many of his colleagues of the time, he aspired to introduce Americans to their vernacular landscape, to teach them to see the common elements of their surroundings—roads, yards, shopping strips, signs, and vacant lots—in a new light. Beyond appreciation and sympathetic understanding of everyday places, such writings help initiate the discovery and appreciation of how ordinary places function and operate. They raise awareness that mundane, generic *spaces* are also *places* we congregate in, are socially engaged with, and above all utilize in our daily routines.

Critics have often compared and contrasted ordinary places with those that invoke historical roots, cultural relations, or unique identity.[3] According to these critics, these generic places, such as airports, shopping malls, highways, or parking lots, cannot generate feelings of belonging, or affectively produce rootedness. Frequently associated with the term "placelessness," these "no-places" have been epitomized by anomie and alienation.

But, is that really the case? Can't the mundane also be valued, appreciated, or become spectacular in its own right?

While ordinary places, such as parking lots, may not be aesthetically pleasing to all, they do serve the purpose they are intended to fulfill, and sometimes a lot more. In the American context, parking lots may be the most common regularly used public outdoor open space. In our automobile-oriented society they are the places one interacts with and uses on a regular basis. They are the places where one may engage in complex social behaviors—traveling, driving, walking, eating, arriving or departing. Parking lots are one of the few places that cars and pedestrians share and coexist in.

Parking lots may be utilitarian and practical, unexceptional, and even unpleasant, but their magnitude and sheer frequency of occurrence merit greater attention. The task is first to rediscover their virtues and common good, and second to elevate their design beyond mediocrity. Even when dealing with the generic, there should be ambition and a desire for perfection.

A PREDICTION WORTH WAITING FOR

In 1991, while being interviewed by an urban planning magazine, renowned landscape architect Peter Walker proclaimed: "The day will come when parking lots routinely win top design honors."[4] That day has yet to materialize. The reality is that surface parking lots have won almost no design competitions or built project awards. For example, since 1990 only one parking lot design has won an award from the American Society of Landscape Architects. The project titled "12,000 Factory Workers Meet Ecology in the Parking Lot, Canton, GA," by Michael Van Valkenburgh Associates, Inc., incorporates innovative stormwater and hydrological techniques with the industrial operation of the adjacent manufacturing facility. The segmented 10-acre parking lot provides spaces for 550 cars and 120 semitrailers. Recycled telephone poles are set within the spaces to provide lighting as well as a visual connection between the surrounding woods and the industrial building.[5]

CARSCAPE

In the mid-1980s a rare parking lot design competition was announced. Sponsored by the City of Columbus, Ohio and the Irwin-Sweeney-Miller Foundation, the challenge was to design a municipal parking lot for about 300 cars, and showcase new approaches that address function and aesthetics. The stated desire was to affect change and "to find a solution intrinsic to the parking function but a step beyond the typical embellishments, e.g., berms, walls, trees etc."[6] Beyond this specific design aim, the larger goal was to expose the deficiencies associated with this particular land use. As stated by the organizers: "The amount of creativity, energy, and planning that goes into the design of these parking places, especially compared to other elements of the built environment, is minuscule. Yet, in terms of their visual impact, their land usage, or any other measure, there is almost no other place of the public environment that people experience more in their daily lives."[7]

The competition received over 130 entries, 36 of which were exhibited and reproduced in *Carscape: A Parking Handbook*, published in 1988 by the Irwin-Sweeney-Miller Foundation.

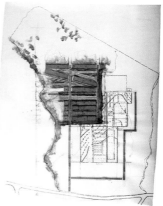

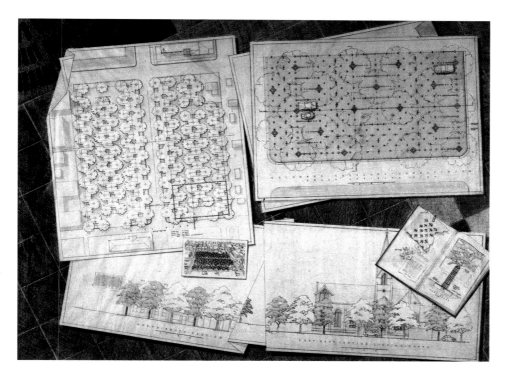

1.3

The parking lot of the Herman Miller furniture
manufacturing and assembly plant in Cherokee
County, Georgia, is one of the few lots to win a design
award. Designed by landscape architect Michael
Van Valkenburgh, it incorporates ecological design
principles to mitigate environmental impacts
such as stormwater runoff while accommodating
over 500 cars and 120 semitrailers. © Michael
Van Valkenburgh

1.4

The winning entry for the Carscape competition in
Columbus, Indiana, by Eric R. Kuhne & Associates,
is described as a transformation of a parking lot
into a park, an urban plaza under a canopy of
trees. Unfortunately, the project was never built.
© CivicArts / Eric R Kuhne & Associates

1.5
Existing standards and reference books are primarily
concerned with spatial dimensions and the amount
of parking spaces provided. Little or no consideration
is given to the design, look, and feel of the lot.
© Jeffrey Smith

The book showcases the entries in terms of their unique approaches to the design of a parking lot, emphasizing multiple uses; landscaping; screens/trellises; parking patterns; and sculptures/monuments.

In summarizing their decision, the jury established the following praiseworthy principles:

- Circulation of automobiles and pedestrians should be simple and direct. It must be easy to use.
- This place should be integrated with the life of the community. It should not be walled off from its surroundings.
- It should accept the automobile for what it is and not try to disguise its power with scenery artifacts.
- Hardedge separation of automobile and pedestrian activity is unnecessary.
- Electric lighting is an essential part of the experience and should form an integral part of the design.
- We encourage the idea of using the parking lot as an urban plaza; the place can also be used without cars.
- The natural landscape should form part of the design. We preferred the confrontation of machines with plants rather than that of machines with architecture or machines with machines.
- Repetitive patterns, not geometric fantasy, are the basic design tool.
- Parking lots represent real estate in transition and should be conceived as a vehicle for change.

The winning entry by Eric R. Kuhne & Associates is described as a transformation of a parking lot into a park, an urban plaza under a canopy of trees. Inspired by the European urban plazas, where lack of space forces the creation of multiuse areas shared by cars, pedestrians, and cultural activities, the result was intended to be "a pleasant place to visit and coexist with cars."[8]

Unfortunately, neither the resulting design nor the competition's principles were embraced or constructed. A brief look at the site today reveals an ordinary asphalt lot dominated by parked cars and paved surfaces.

SETTING THE BAR

The *Wiley Graphic Standards*, a guidebook typically used as a reference for practitioners and students, publishes in its Student Edition a paltry four-page section on parking lots. Out of the four pages only three short paragraphs of text complement typical drawings of standardized parking layouts. The first sentence on parking lot design is: "Parking lots should offer direct and easy access for people walking between their vehicles and the building entrances."[9] No mention is made of the overall integration of the parking lot with the surroundings, or its aesthetic quality. It is noted: "when possible, parking lots should be designed to have reduced paved areas, to minimize runoff problems, and to provide areas for trees and other vegetation."[10] This is the sum of all the guidance on parking design provided to students in a 436-page book on urban design and planning. It is unfortunate that in a manual used to supplement design and planning education, less than 1 percent is dedicated to the design of parking lots, which occupy up to 40 percent of our urban land. If we do not begin teaching students how to design better parking lots, including design theory, then we should not be disappointed when parking lots are disregarded in practice.

DEMAND

ZONED

As long as cars exist, they will continue to occupy space. This space will have to be provided whether it is required by law or by need. In the United States, parking requirements are typically tied to zoning regulations. Suggestions for off-street parking standards as part of urban planning-zoning strategy started to appear in the early 1930s.[11] At that time, with zoning being a newly minted instrument of urban planning and development control, it was seen as the easiest way to directly make property owners contribute to solving the on-street parking problem. Parking thus became a perpetual, legally binding element of development, as have more conventional requirements such as fire safety and sanitation infrastructure provisions.

RATIOS

How many parking spaces does one need to provide? Since the early 1980s city officials have relied on the Institute of Transportation Engineers (ITE) handbooks—*Trip Generation* and *Parking Genera-tion*—to estimate the number of required parking spaces for a particular development. These two books have had a tremendous influence on the way our cities and towns look, feel, and operate. By suggesting peak parked vehicles per unit of particular land use (for example, 4 parking spaces per 1,000 gross square feet [93 square meters], dwelling unit, employee, etc.), ITE has created a formula that is used in most transportation models, travel forecasts, planning decisions, municipal ordinances, and court rulings.[12] These numbers are then translated to either paved surfaces or structured parking.

Unfortunately, and like many other standards and codes generated by engineers, policy makers and urban planners often take these parking calculations for granted. ITE's stamp of authority relieves public officials of any obligation to figure things out for themselves, or to take responsibility for the urban form and built environment that these numbers generate. Various studies suggest that parking is often oversupplied in both residential and commercial areas. Zoning codes typically require between three and five spaces per 1,000 gross square feet of building area, with four spaces per thousand feet building used as a rule of thumb.[13] Some independent parking surveys, however, show that even at peak demand level, only two to three spaces per 1,000 square feet are utilized. A case study of a suburban office building in Southern California found parking was oversupplied by factor of almost two. The average amount of parking supply was at 3.8 spaces per 1,000 square feet, but only 2.1 spaces were used during peak times. Another survey of parking demand at neighborhood commercial lots in Iowa, during the ten-day period before Christmas, found the highest parking occupancy rate was 74 percent.[14]

Criticism and challenges to prevailing parking ratio formulas have had little impact and have resulted in insignificant changes. In his paper "Truth in Transportation Planning," Donald Shoup argues that urban transportation engineers often use precise numbers to report uncertain estimates. By carefully studying the variables used to calculate parking spaces, Shoup shows that "it would be hard to find two variables that are more unrelated than floor area and parking demand." Nevertheless, ITE reports the average parking generation rate for a fast food restaurant, for example, as precisely 9.95 parking spaces per 1,000 square feet. Shoup continues: "I do not suggest that parking demand and vehicle trips are unrelated to a restaurant's floor area. Commonsense tells us that there is some relationship, but we should recognize that the ITE data do not show a statistically significant relationship between floor area and either parking demand or vehicle trips."[15]

MINIMAL DESIGN

Whether one designs parking spaces for five or for fifty cars, the quality and physical design of the spaces themselves is hardly discussed or enforced through regulations. While parking lot aesthetics were seen as an important element during the early days of parking lot design (1920s–1940s), in the present day they seem to be left to the discretion of the developer.

Surprisingly, some of the most progressive cities in the United States hardly stipulate how a surface parking lot should look. Cambridge, Massachusetts, for example, has sophisticated parking regulations which include over 30 pages of ways to measure the number of parking spaces, and the parking provision, required for each land use category. In the opening page, the regulations state: "The parking standards contained herein are intended to encourage public transit, bicycle usage and walking in lieu of automobiles where a choice of travel mode exists. It is also the purpose of this Article to allow flexibility in providing required parking through shared or off-site arrangements in order to accommodate the automobile in the urban environment in a less disruptive way. Development regulations and design standards have been established to reduce hazard to pedestrians on public sidewalks, to ensure the usefulness of parking and loading facilities, and where appropriate, to avoid potential adverse impacts on adjacent land uses, and to enhance the visual quality of the city."[16]

Indeed, and as reflected in this statement, parking lots are seen as unsightly elements in the urban fabric, which need to be mitigated. Rather than approaching lot creation as an opportunity to integrate attractive places, the regulations are primarily concerned with buffering and concealing a parking lot from neighbors and passersby. Section 6.47 states: "Off-street parking facilities containing five or more spaces and not in a structure shall be effectively screened from abutting streets and lots. However, such screening shall not obstruct vehicle sight distances, entrances and exits." Other provisions include minimum tree coverage (one tree per 10 parking spaces), detailed dimensions for setbacks and stalls, and general recommendations for paving.

FUNCTIONAL

The relation of form to function is often debated in the design and architecture field.[17] Whether architecture or design styles follow one or the other, parking lots are the spaces that can easily straddle the line between *form* (elegance, grace, and beauty) and *function* (usability, dependability, and value). Parking lots are a *type* of place, so ordinary and familiar that we ignore their existence until we need them. Yet it is in this everyday amorphous, banal, and repetitive collection of functional and utilitarian areas that an opportunity for change exists.

TYPE

The utilitarian and mechanical nature of parking has resulted in a specific and distinct array of spatial shapes and patterns. Incorporated into the full spectrum of human settlement, from the most rural to the most urban, and servicing the gamut of architectural construction, from homes to big box retail, certain types of lots have emerged. Their taxonomy can be useful in trying to address design techniques or particular deficiencies. Lots can be classified according to what types of parking one can expect to find in different realms of rural to suburban and urban areas, or according to size, starting from the smallest footprint to the largest. For example, in "Seeking Urbane Parking Solutions," Brian O'Looney and Neal Payton offer a typology of parking solutions along a transect of development from the lowest levels of urban density to the highest.[18]

1.6

Boston, Massachusetts. Since the 1930s, parking requirements in the United States have typically been tied to zoning regulations. © Massachusetts Institute of Technology, Courtesy of MIT Libraries, Rotch Visual Collections; Photograph by Nishan Bichajian

1.7

Maricopa County, Arizona. Most parking regulations rely on trip generation formulas to calculate the number of required parking spaces for a particular development, for example 4 parking spaces per 1,000 gross square feet (93 square meters) of office space. These numbers, correct or not, are then translated to paved surfaces. © Alan Berger

1.8

Marlborough, Massachusetts. Parking lots are often built to accommodate the anticipated crowd of customers on the busiest shopping days of the year. As a result, a typical single-story commercial building requires a minimum of one-half to three-quarters (more typical) of the site dedicated to parking. © Alan Berger

PARKING LOT TYPOLOGIES

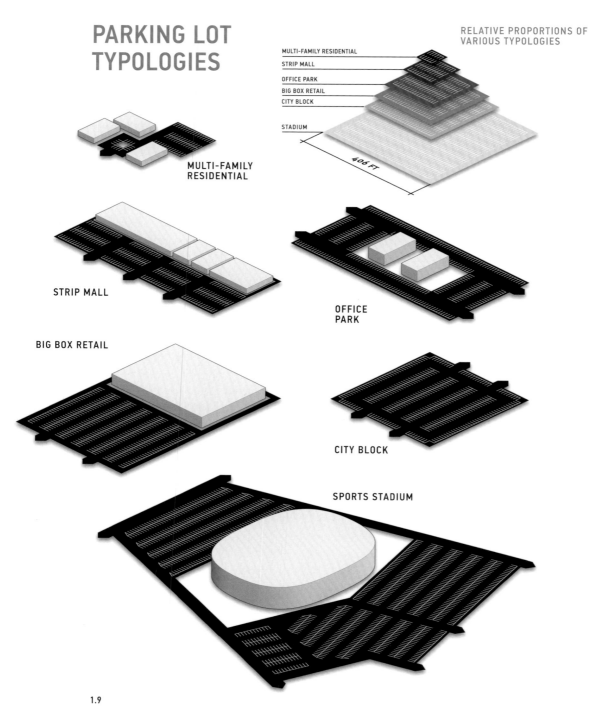

RELATIVE PROPORTIONS OF
VARIOUS TYPOLOGIES

MULTI-FAMILY RESIDENTIAL
STRIP MALL
OFFICE PARK
BIG BOX RETAIL
CITY BLOCK
STADIUM

406 FT

MULTI-FAMILY
RESIDENTIAL

STRIP MALL

OFFICE
PARK

BIG BOX RETAIL

CITY BLOCK

SPORTS STADIUM

1.9

Parking lot typologies identify a cross-section of
the lots one may find in rural, suburban, and urban
areas, from the smallest footprint to the largest.
There are many ways any one type of lot can be
designed; the diagrams are intended to give a typical
example of each. © Stephen Kennedy

SPACE OF DIMENSIONS

A typical parking space is 8–10 feet (2.5–3.0 meters) wide and 18–20 feet (5.5–6.0 meters) long, totaling 144–200 square feet (13–19 square meters). Add to it access lanes and minimal landscaping, and the space required to accommodate one car increases to 300–350 square feet (28–32 square meters). A one-acre lot will provide space for about 100–150 cars (250–370 per hectare), depending on its design and the amount of green areas.[19] But how many such parking spaces are there?

No nationwide inventory of parking in the United States exists. However, several researchers have attempted to estimate total area of parking based on regulatory parking requirements and evaluations of aerial imagery. Most of these studies are either local in nature or do not differentiate between various types of parking such as off-street lots or multistory garages. As such, they tend to vary greatly. For example, a study using aerial photographs to estimate the number of parking spaces in surface lots in Illinois, Indiana, Michigan, and Wisconsin identified more than 43 million parking spaces. This translates to approximately 2.5 to 3.0 off-street, nonresidential parking spaces per vehicle.[20] Some studies even suggest that if you include on-street parking, U.S. cities have an average of about of eight parking spaces for each car.[21]

Since the measuring techniques and resulting parking figures varied considerably, researchers at the University of California at Berkeley attempted to compile all previous analyses and develop new figures. They examined estimated numbers based on five different scenarios. The first scenario is based on the conservative estimate of 105 million pay-parking spaces reported by the International Parking Institute. The next three scenarios examine what the researchers consider to be the most likely situation: known inventory, available survey data, and regulations and standards. The fifth scenario evaluates the extreme upper end where the rule-of-thumb ratio of 8 spaces to 1 car is employed.[22] The averaged results show between 105 million and 2.0 billion total parking spaces in the United States, out of which 36 million to 790 million are in off-street surface lots.

While the first case is the most conservative of the scenarios, and the last one is the most extreme, even the middle ground of about 500 million spaces is staggering. If all of those spaces were consolidated into a single location, they would cover an area of about 3,590 square miles (9,300 square kilometers), or a bit larger than the size of Puerto Rico (based on a very modest 200 square feet [18.6 square meters] per vehicle).

WALKMOBILIE

Hermann Knoflacher, an Austrian civil engineer, created the *Walkmobilie* in the mid-1970s. With simple materials strapped around his body, Knoflacher compared the actual physical space one driver occupies while in a vehicle as opposed to one person walking. The mathematician and architect Christopher Alexander speaks to the same notion: "The problems [of vast parking lots] stem essentially from the fact that a car is so much bigger than a person. Large parking lots, suited for the cars, have all the wrong properties for people. They are too wide; they contain too much pavement; they have no place to linger."[23]

CAR AND WORK

The American Community Survey estimates that for the year 2009, 94.5 percent of the country's population drives by private car to work (for people over the age of 16), 83.5 percent in single-occupancy vehicles and 11 percent in carpools.[24] Combining the 105,476,045 single-occupancy vehicles and the 13,916,694 cars for the carpooling (assuming two persons per car for the carpool), a total estimate of 119,392,739 cars were used for daily commuting, according to the Survey. Assuming 119,000,000

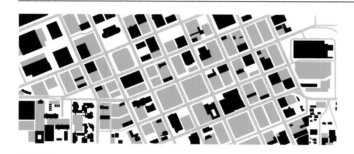

SMALL TOWN MAIN STREET
PULASKI, VA

15%

19%

6%

NEW ENGLAND TOWN CENTER
CHELMSFORD, MA

27%

12%

6%

MIDTOWN/ DOWNTOWN
TULSA, OK

28%

21%

15%

SUBURBAN STRIP
ORLANDO, FL

36%

22%

9%

1.10

Diagrams showing typical urban conditions in the United
States and surface parking lots' coverage.

Orange: surface parking
Black: building's footprint
Gray: roads
White: unpaved areas

© Stephen Kennedy

1.11
Hermann Knoflacher, an Austrian civil engineer,
created the *Walkmobilie* to demonstrate the
actual physical space one driver occupies while
in a vehicle as opposed to one person walking.
© Institut für Verkehrsplanung und Verkehrstechnik,
TU Wien

cars as a base, this translates to 23,800,000,000 square feet (2,211,092,352 square meters) of space required for parking vehicles at work, based on a very modest 200 square feet (18.6 square meters) per vehicle. (This does not include the space needed for maneuvering, and travel lanes to the parking spaces.) In addition, each of these cars also came from somewhere. Multiplying 23,800,000,000 by two, we get 47,600,000,000 square feet of parking area. This conservative estimate shows these cars would occupy about 1,093,000 acres or about 1,700 square miles (4,400 square kilometers) of land if they were all housed in surface parking lots. This is about 75 times the area of Manhattan and slightly larger than the total area of the state of Rhode Island.

RATIOS TO SPACE

The consequences of required parking demand ratios, city codes, and retail-driven standards are evident throughout the American landscape. Shopping malls, directed by anchor stores, typically specify one parking space for every 225 square feet or 4.5 spaces per 1,000 square feet (21 square meters) of gross leasable area. Many municipalities require one space per 75 square feet for restaurants (12 spaces per 1,000 square feet). At a minimum, a typical single-story commercial building requires a minimum one-half to a more typical three-quarters of a site to be dedicated to parking. For a two-story building, close to 80 percent of a site must be set aside for surface parking.

Furthermore, it is well known that developers build parking lots to accommodate the anticipated crowd of customers on the busiest shopping day of the year—the day after Thanksgiving. Similarly, church parking lots are often designed to accommodate Christmas and Easter services. As a result, a whole lot of land gets paved over—over and over again—that doesn't have to be.

"ARE YOU CRAZY? I CAN NEVER FIND PARKING WHERE I'M GOING!"

Although ample physical space is provided for parking, our cultural and psychological perception is typically the contrary. In Tippecanoe County, Indiana, there are 250,000 more parking spaces than registered cars and trucks. That means that if every driver left home at the same time and parked at the local minimarts, grocery stores, churches, and schools, a quarter of a million spaces would still be standing empty. The county's parking lots take up more land than 1,000 football fields, covering more than two square miles, and that's not counting the driveways of homes or parking spots on the street. In a county of 155,000 inhabitants, there are 11 parking spaces for every family. Bryan Pijanowski, a professor of forestry and natural resources at Purdue University, which is located in Tippecanoe, documented the parking bounty in a research study. When it made the news, Pijanowski got puzzled reactions from locals. In short, they said: "Are you crazy? I can never find parking where I'm going!"[25]

THE BEST PARKING SPACE

What is the best strategy for selecting a "good" parking spot? Much depends on the condition of the lot, and one's definition of "good." If it is crowded, one jumps into the first open spot—no matter where it is or how inconvenient it might be. At other off-peak times, people seek a spot that is closest to their destination, and while doing so will cruise the aisles multiple times searching for the best space, waiting for cars to leave.

But is one way more efficient than another? According to an article published in the journal *Transportation Science* titled "A Probabilistic Approach to Evaluate Strategies for Selecting a Parking Space Source," there is. In the study, the authors, Cassady and Kobza, used a probabilistic approach to evaluate space-seeking strategies, treating driver decisions and parking space availability as random experiments in a "typical" parking lot (four entries, seven rows with 72 spaces each, handicapped parking, employee spaces, shopping cart return locations, and directional restrictions).

The researchers considered three performance measures of what constitutes a "good" parking spot: the total walking distance between the space and the mall's entrance doors (including distance walked to the door, back to the car after shopping, and to return a shopping cart); drive time in search of a space; and the amount of time to reach the front door after entering the lot. Their comparison showed that in their model, the "park and walk" approach takes an average of 61 seconds from entering the lot to reaching the mall entrance, whereas the "cruising" strategy requires an average of 71 seconds. The first approach usually involves more walking, but one tends to start shopping sooner and maybe even burn few calories at the same time.[26]

CHINA AND THE WORLD

In April 2010, Rao Da, general secretary of the China Passenger Car Association, announced that by the end of 2010 China's vehicle sales would surpass 17 million, growing by about 25 percent. According to international experience, when average per capita GDP hits about $1,000, a country will start to see households purchasing cars. In 2001, when China's per capita GDP passed the $1,000 mark, households had already started to purchase cars. The number of family car purchases each year from 2003 to 2007 was consecutively 1,780,000, 2,000,000, 2,930,000, 4,110,000, and 4,930,000—an increase of around 1,000,000 every year. In 2009, according to the normal progression, 7,000,000 cars should have been sold. However, as a result of auto purchase subsidies, and pent-up demand from 2008, the number of cars sold in 2009 was 8,500,000. It is estimated that in 2010 around 60,000,000 passenger cars were occupying roads and parking spots in China.

According to the World Bank 2010 *World Development Indicators*, the United States still leads the ranks in the numbers of cars per population: 814 cars for every 1,000 people for a total of 249,903,698, with Qatar and Australia ranking second and third. When calculating the density of cars per square mile (or square kilometer), the Netherlands comes up on top with 246 vehicles per square kilometer (0.38 square mile), followed by Japan and Belgium.

COST AND CONSEQUENCES

ASPHALT DEFINED

Surface parking lots are cheap to build. In 2008 it was estimated that the average per-space cost of surface parking was $4,000, versus $20,000 in an above-grade parking structure and $30,000–$40,000 in an underground garage.[27]

However, within that low cost average, construction costs for surface lots vary dramatically, based on land acquisition costs and other contextual constraints. For that reason, costs for surface parking lots can range from near nothing to over $10,000 per space (based on calculating the average space needed for one car parking stall, maneuvering space of 300 square feet, and estimated land valued at $50 per square foot).[28]

FINANCIAL COSTS

It is estimated that the annual cost of all parking spaces (garage, surface, and curb) equals that of car ownership, though vehicle expenses are typically paid by owners, while the parking costs are spread out over a more complicated system of support.[29]

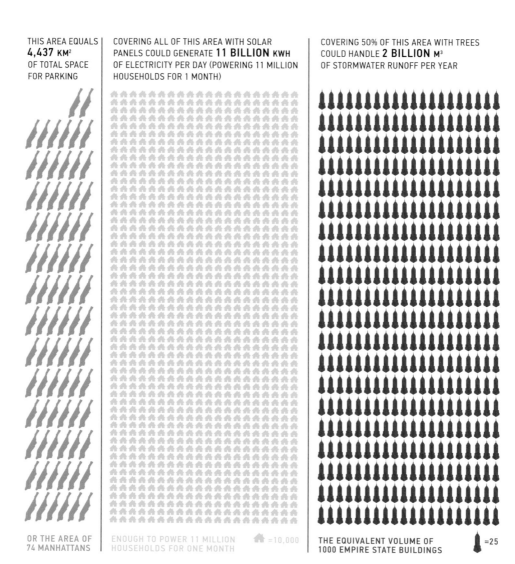

THIS AREA EQUALS
4,437 KM²
OF TOTAL SPACE
FOR PARKING

COVERING ALL OF THIS AREA WITH SOLAR
PANELS COULD GENERATE **11 BILLION** KWH
OF ELECTRICITY PER DAY (POWERING 11 MILLION
HOUSEHOLDS FOR 1 MONTH)

COVERING 50% OF THIS AREA WITH TREES
COULD HANDLE **2 BILLION** M³
OF STORMWATER RUNOFF PER YEAR

OR THE AREA OF
74 MANHATTANS

ENOUGH TO POWER 11 MILLION
HOUSEHOLDS FOR ONE MONTH   = 10,000

THE EQUIVALENT VOLUME OF
1000 EMPIRE STATE BUILDINGS   = 25

1.12

Comparative space consumption diagram of land
utilized in the United States for parking cars.
A conservative estimate shows that cars would
occupy 1,096,352 acres or 1,713 square miles
(4,437 square kilometers) of land if they were all
housed in surface parking lots. © Stephen Kennedy

COVERING 50% OF THIS AREA WITH TREES
COULD GENERATE **822,264** TONS OF
OXYGEN PER YEAR

COVERING 50% OF THIS AREA WITH TREES
COULD REMOVE **1,260,805** TONS OF
CARBON DIOXIDE PER YEAR

WEIGHT OF ABOUT 5,500
BLUE WHALES   = 22

WEIGHT OF ABOUT 20,000
AFRICAN ELEPHANTS   = 25

1.13
© Eran Ben-Joseph

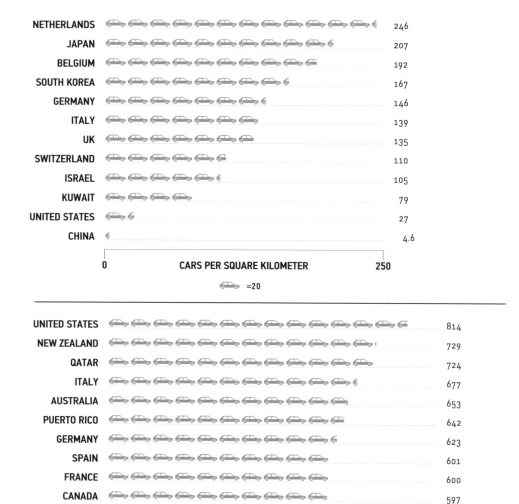

NETHERLANDS		246
JAPAN		207
BELGIUM		192
SOUTH KOREA		167
GERMANY		146
ITALY		139
UK		135
SWITZERLAND		110
ISRAEL		105
KUWAIT		79
UNITED STATES		27
CHINA		4.6

0   CARS PER SQUARE KILOMETER   250

= 20

UNITED STATES		814
NEW ZEALAND		729
QATAR		724
ITALY		677
AUSTRALIA		653
PUERTO RICO		642
GERMANY		623
SPAIN		601
FRANCE		600
CANADA		597
JAPAN		595
NORWAY		572
CHINA		32

0   CARS PER 1000 PEOPLE   900

= 60

1.14

Cars and nations comparisons. Source:
The World Bank 2010 *World Development
Indicators*. © Stephen Kennedy

The financial cost of providing new areas of parking is driven by three key factors: the number of parking spaces required, the opportunity cost of the land to be used for parking, and the cost per parking space.

- Parking requirements that assume suburban levels of demand in urban locations may necessitate large surface lots or parking garages, unnecessarily increasing the cost of infill housing and other compact development.

- The opportunity cost is the cost of using a space for parking instead of a use with higher value. This varies considerably depending on the development context. In infill locations, the opportunity cost can be quite high, as each on-site parking space can reduce the number of new housing units or other uses by 25 percent or more.[30] The cost per space also depends on engineering and design considerations, as well as the land, construction, maintenance, utilities, insurance, administrative, and operating costs. The per-space costs tend to be higher in infill locations, providing a strong incentive for avoiding a parking surplus.[31]

1.15
It is estimated that in 2010, around 60,000,000 passenger cars were occupying roads and parking spots in China. © Samuel Rosenberg

1.16

Mira Loma, California. Surface parking lots are cheap to build. Asphalt lots do not only accommodate shoppers and dwellers, but are also the primary source of surface parking for heavy industry, manufacturing, and commerce. © Alan Berger

DANGER: PARKING PAL MAGNET

Nearly half of all pedestrian accidents involving children aged one to four occur when a vehicle is backing up in a driveway. According to a national advocacy organization, Kids and Cars, approximately 50 children are injured or killed every year as a result of vehicles backing up (40 percent of non-traffic-related fatalities involve children younger than 15). The number of back-over deaths has actually increased in recent years. From 2002 through 2006, 474 children died compared with 128 deaths reported during the period from 1997 to 2001. Research has shown that children in this age range are simply too young to understand the dangers of a moving vehicle.

Although this number (50) is high, it is relatively low compared to the hundreds of pedestrians younger than 15 who are killed each year by cars (in 2008, 875 pedestrian fatalities). To combat the rising death toll of children in back-over accidents, Congress recently enacted the Cameron Gulbransen Act.[32] The Act was named for two-year-old Cameron Gulbransen, who was killed when he was inadvertently backed over by an SUV because the vehicle's blind spot made it impossible for the driver to see him. The Act directs the United States Department of Transportation to adopt new safety standards that will lead to the design and development of safety technologies to prevent injuries and death to children caused by back-over accidents. In time these improvements will become standard equipment in all vehicles.[33]

The fear of back-over accidents in parking lots has also generated a few commercial safety gadgets. The Parking Pal magnet is one. The palm-sized, brightly colored, flat, hand-shaped magnet is placed on the side of the car. As children exit the car they place their hand on the patch to remain in one place while waiting for the adult to lead them from the side of the vehicle. According to the commercial distributor, "children love to place their hands on [it]. After a couple of learning sessions, [the] child will discover that the Parking Pal is their safe spot, and they will know where to go the second they are outside the car. It also helps teach them that parking lots are no place to play."

I SAW AN ANT IN A PARKING LOT

The description of parking lots as bleak, unforgiving, and uninteresting places is passed on to children at an early age. The children's book *I Saw an Ant in a Parking Lot* tells the story of Dorothy Mott, the ticket matron of a parking lot. She is a self-described lot attendant, with duties of "gather[ing] tickets, punch[ing] the clock, and help[ing] lost parkers find their spots."[34] A minivan comes into the lot, looking for a spot, and Dot (Dorothy) recognizes an ant is in trouble: "Now minivans are surely not / a mini-peril / when you've got / a mini-ant out on a trot / across a mega parking lot."[35] Racked with fear for the ant's life, Dot throws a doughnut across the lot as a warning sign to the mother driving

1.17

The fear of children having accidents in parking lots has generated a few commercial safety gadgets. The Parking Pal magnet is one such idea. The palm-sized, brightly colored, flat, hand-shaped magnet is placed on the side of the car. As children exit the car they place their hand on the patch to remain in one place while waiting for the adult to lead them away.
© Denise Whitney

the van. She is successful, as "that sticky missile / hit the spot / just east of anguish, west of caught / north of trouble, south of shot." [36] In the end, disaster is avoided, and all is in place: "Score: Dorothy 1, disaster naught! / An ant alive, / a van in spot! / A doughnut shared and coffee hot. / All is well in Dorothy's lot." [37] This story, bright with illustrations which depict the scary, dangerous world of the parking lot, help create the preconditions for young children to be afraid of surface lots.

RIGHT NEXT TO YOU

Another book, *Parking Lot Rules & 75 Other Ideas for Raising Amazing Children*, promotes the same conclusion but gears its message toward a different consumer—the parent. In his book about how to raise children with respect and love, Tom Sturges deals with "everyday" rules; the first chapter in this section (in theory the most important everyday rule for raising your child) begins with a word of caution: "In a world inhabited by cars the size of small houses, the parking lot can be an incredibly dangerous place." [38] This short passage includes a description of why parking lots are among the most dangerous places:

> Teach your children Parking Lot Rules, that they need to be right next to you always and whenever you are in a parking lot. There is to be no trailing behind. No racing ahead. No exceptions. Right next to you.

> The moment you near a parking lot, either to or from the car, call out "Parking Lot Rules" and your children will know that they absolutely must be by your side. If they have toys in their hands, or Game Boys, or PSPs, or (if you're lucky) a good book, it gets put away that instant.

> Nothing is more important than their walking next to you, holding your hand, and safely getting back and forth from the car. . . . Shout out "Parking lot Rules." Your children will know instantly and instinctively that they need to be by your side, that instant, no questions asked. [39]

Somehow parenting advice for raising an amazing child has to do with keeping him or her alive in surface parking lots. Whether one decides to throw doughnuts to avoid disaster or have a code word for one's children to keep by one's side, we can be sure that the common conception of surface parking lots is that they are dangerous, scary places for small children.

PARTY: TEENAGE FREEDOM

Part of growing up requires testing limits and pushing the envelope of rules and orders—and parking lots seem to be a favorite place to do it. Children learning to ride bicycles, teenagers learning how to drive with a nervous parent alongside, and the teenage pastime of parking for intimate experience in remote areas are all cultural associations to lots. Objects of nostalgia within the American landscape, these places hark back to the time when parking lots held the potential to be special social places.

Similarly, parking lots in many urban and suburban areas are often used for nighttime parties; many parking lots outside clubs draw large crowds of people who have no intention of entering the club but, rather, come for the party outside. The popularity of parking lot parties is so great that one recent music video (by the artist Trae) was almost entirely shot at a parking lot party. [40] Parties in parking lots have been popularized in such songs as Jay-Z's "Parking Lot Pimping."

Thus, the parking lot is the place to be. The music video by Trae had been viewed on YouTube 2,393,278 times as of February 2011. [41] The result, whether intended or not, is that millions of people watching the video have the association that parking lots are where celebrities hang out, where the party is at, and are cool places to be.

1.18

Photographer Rachel Feierman captures the drama
of youth as it plays out at night in parking lots across
the country. Young people come to flirt, socialize,
show off their cars, and compete. During the off hours,
when stores are closed and local police are otherwise
occupied, the empty space is theirs. Commandeered
from main street, the strip mall lots have become a
modern stage, empty, theatrically lit, and available
for play. © Rachel Feierman

1.19

Portland, Oregon. Food trucks and parking lots enjoy
a symbiotic relationship. From traditional hot dogs
to sophisticated ethnic cuisine, one can enjoy a
quickly served fresh meal in a convenient location.
© Sarah Snider

LOTS OF EATING

Food trucks can be found everywhere. Parked along the side of roads or at the edge of parking lots, they sell every imaginable food type. From simple hot dogs to sophisticated ethnic cuisine, one can enjoy a quickly served fresh meal in a convenient location. Food trucks and parking enjoy a symbiotic relationship. While food trucks cannot exist without a parking space, their existence enlivens the space and supports an economic base. A number of cities and local vendors have pushed this relationship between space and activity to become an event. In Somerville, Massachusetts, the Arts Council, a steward of an arts-based economic development strategy, came up with the idea of "Brunch in the Square." Somerville Arts Council Executive Director Greg Jenkins saw the potential of creating a more permanent yet still temporary (weekly variety) event to make use of the parking lot at the city's Union Square to encourage activity in the area. He suggested local food truck vendors come into the square from 10:00 a.m. to 3:00 p.m. on Sundays and set up small movable chairs and tables for people to come and have brunch, using part of the parking lot as the outside dining room.[42]

In California, the Southern California Mobile Food Vendors Association (SCMFVA) is trying to establish a new trend for food trucks—permanent spaces for mobile eateries to share. They have joined forces with parking lot owners around Los Angeles to provide spaces for food trucks in various locations around the city. Another group, the Santa Monica Gourmet Food Truck Corner, is aimed at serving clients from 11 a.m. to 8 p.m., Monday through Saturday, on an empty parking lot. Seven to eight trucks are to be on rotation six days a week with half the trucks serving during the lunch rush, the other half for dinner. Diners can follow the trucks on the various lots around Los Angeles on any given day using Web interfaces like Twitter. Future plans for many of these lots include adding tables, chairs, WiFi, special dog areas, and bicycle parking.

TAILGATES

The Web site tailgating.com greets one with the slogan "Welcome to the celebration in the parking lot!"[43] The site is run and managed by Joe Cahn, aka the "Commissioner of Tailgating." A native of New Orleans, Joe left a career in cooking and started his journey through stadiums' pregame parking lots looking for specialty cooking by tailgaters. Since starting his journey in 1996, Joe has visited over 650 tailgating games on an 800,000-mile, 15-season journey.[44]

For Joe, as well as for the thousands who tailgate every week, the parking lot is their home and their neighborhood. "It's the last great American neighborhood," Joe proclaims, "the tailgating neighborhood. Where no one locks their doors, everyone is happy to see you and all are together sharing fun, food and football! It's families. It's fans. It's a community social."[45]

The roots of the popular pastime of tailgating can be traced back to the first intercollegiate American football games. Some claim tailgating started at the first game between Rutgers and Princeton in 1869, where fans in horse-drawn carriages grilled sausages at the "tail end" of the wagon.[46] The popularity of tailgating increased after World War II, with fans using popular station wagons to set up cooking grills. In the 1980s and 1990s tailgating groups formed into communities with group names and even group flags.

Whatever its origin, tailgating in the lot has become an official part of the American football pregame experience. Rules for tailgate parking and parking lot behavior are an integral part of sport teams and stadium managements. Most of the National Football League stadiums post the hours when parking lots are open (usually four hours before and one hour after game time), set up rules for tailgating, and provide specific areas within the lots for the use of tailgaters. The San Francisco 49ers, for example, have clear diagrams showing the correct setup for tailgaters, including location of car, table, BBQ, and canopy, that must be adhered to.

Eating, drinking, mingling, and socializing in a parking lot have also created an opportunity for community building and economic development. College athletic programs, coaches, parents and players often use parking lot tailgating to enhance team spirit and to fundraise. Mainstream media set up portable stages in parking lots to create a tailgate atmosphere and to broadcast pregame shows. The idea of pregame and preshow activities has also reached festivals and concerts within the arts community. One can find black-tie events with wine and preconcert entertainment before the opening night performance of the Santa Fe Opera and, conversely, the laid-back tropical-themed gatherings of margarita-drinking, parrot-hatted fans partying before Jimmy Buffett concerts.

1.20

Tailgating in the lot has become an official part of American football where eating, drinking, and socializing have became a common pregame experience. Some stadium Web sites have tailgate diagrams that show the correct setup for cars, tables, BBQs, and canopies that tailgaters must adhere to. © Wakemily

1.21

Many Walmart stores welcome campers and recreation vehicles to overnight for free in their parking lots. Managers reason that the distant outer reaches of their vast lots are unlikely to ever be occupied, and that the campers constitute a customer base since they are likely to stock up on necessary merchandise while in the lot. © Lynnette Walczak

BOONDOCKING

The term "boondocking" is an adapted form of an adapted word. "Boondock" comes from the Tagalog word *bundok*, meaning "mountain." It entered the English language at some time during World War II, when American soldiers in the Philippines used it to mean "remote and wild place." Next it morphed into a verb: "boondocking," to camp in the wilderness. In recent years, its usage has evolved further still, and today "boondock" wilderness might be a Walmart parking lot.

A sizable community of recreation vehicle (RV) owners has taken to parking in Walmart lots overnight, as a free alternative to established RV parks. The Web site boondocking.org, for example, provides a nationwide database of parking lots suitable for boondocking, complete with GPS coordinates.

Though policies vary from store to store, many Walmarts welcome these "boondockers." Managers reason that the distant outer reaches of their vast lots are unlikely to ever be occupied anyway, and that the boondockers constitute a new customer base, as they shop and stock up on necessary merchandise.

For many RVers, it seems, boondocking is not just a way to save a few dollars, but an expression of independence. It offers the best of both worlds—the feeling of being in a lonely, windswept frontier while moving, and the convenience of 24-hour shopping while parking. "We've seen people sitting around the asphalt telling campfire stories," said a Walmart spokesperson. "They pull up their camp chairs, pull out their awnings."[47] Out somewhere beyond the shopping cart return, they are at home on the range.

(BOONDOCKING) ECONOMICS

There may be big money in parking lots. After Nova Scotia passed a province-wide ban on staying overnight in parking lots, a retired economist and avid RVer, Andrew Cornwall, prepared (on his own initiative) a 66-page report for the Nova Scotia Department of Tourism, Culture and Heritage assessing the ban's economic impact. He found that Nova Scotia was being crippled by the ban and the accompanying reputation of being "RV-unfriendly." According to survey evidence, removing the ban could increase RV tourism in the province by up to 83 percent. Such an increase would result in an extra 906 person-years of employment annually for Nova Scotia's economy, and generate $6.3 million in provincial and $1.4 million in municipal tax revenues.[48]

The government, perhaps convinced by his report, repealed the ban in June 2010.

1.22

Located in almost all major shopping center parking
lots in the 1980s, Fotomat was a brilliant business
venture. The kiosks required a minimal amount of land
and employees (usually one per kiosk), and clients
were able to drive up to drop off or pick up film without
needing to park or get out of their vehicle. Courtesy
Fotomat Co.

1.23

Mary Ellis's grave in New Brunswick, New Jersey.
Strangely enough, few shopping mall parking
lots have been developed around burial grounds.
The coexistence of these land uses—graves, parking,
and retail—shows the importance of parking to
the American shopper. (Another noted site is a Native
American burial ground in a strip mall parking lot
in Sand Springs, Oklahoma.) © Jonathan Lansey

FOTOMAT

With their distinctive pyramid-shaped gold-colored roofs and bright red lettering, these little kiosks adorned over 4,000 parking lots. A retail chain of one-day photo development, the drive-through business format reached its peak in the 1980s. Located in almost all major shopping center parking lots, Fotomat was a brilliant business venture. The kiosks required a minimal amount of land and number of employees (usually one per kiosk), and clients were able to drive up to drop off or pick up film without needing to park or get out of their vehicle.

With the introduction of one-hour photo development, and later on digital photography and self-printing, Fotomat kiosks and their appeal became obsolete. By the late 1980s the company was sold and eventually moved its operation to Internet-based photo storage. By 2009 its Web site was closed as well. Remnants of Fotomat kiosks can be seen in many parking lots, often taken over by small local entrepreneurs to use as drive-through coffee, cigarette, or flower kiosks.

GRAVE LOT

The parking lot in front of the Loews Theater in New Brunswick, New Jersey is entirely unremarkable, except for one thing. Smack in the middle lies a small elevated plateau containing the grave of Mary Ellis. Mary has been in this location since her death in 1827. When she chose the site, it lay amid bucolic woodlands overlooking the Raritan River (where she had waited in vain for many years for her sea captain lover to return). Through it all, Mary has managed to hold on to her spot, giving new meaning to the phrase "long-term parking."

Suffice it to say, Mary could never have anticipated what would happen in the future. The surrounding property passed from one owner to the next, until it was paved over in the twentieth century. Fronting onto Route 1, the site was destined to be exploited for its commercial potential.

ON THE LOT

From providing the location for destroying a police car by strapping a cable to the rear bumper in *American Graffiti* to the pile-up of cars after a chase scene in the James Bond movie *Diamonds Are Forever*, parking lots have starred in major films and commercials. One of the most memorable parking lot movie scenes belongs to "Towanda," the parking lot warrior. Actress Kathy Bates, in the 1991 film *Fried Green Tomatoes*, has immortalized in it the ultimate parking lot rage scene. Bates, portraying Evelyn, a middle-aged insecure woman, is patiently waiting in her large American car for a parking space to open up when two snappy young women zoom their red convertible Volkswagen Beetle into it before she can react. When Evelyn tells the two disembarking girls that she had been waiting for that spot, they scoff at her, saying dismissively while walking away: "Face it, lady. We're younger and faster." In a classic display of indignation, Evelyn utters the word "Towanda," hits the gas pedal to the floor and rams their car several times, causing extensive damage. When the young girls run out of the grocery store screaming: "What are you doing? Are you crazy?," Evelyn casually replies, while driving away victoriously: "Face it, girls, I'm older and I have more insurance."

Unlike the random parking scenes in Hollywood movies, *The Parking Lot Movie* is a full feature documentary devoted to a small lot in Charlottesville, Virginia and the various parking attendants who work there. In a mix of interviews and monologues the attendants talk about their interaction with cars, drivers, and the erratic behavior associated with paid parking. The lot, in their eyes, becomes a metaphor, a mirror of society and cultural behavior. As one attendant proclaims: "The parking lot was the place where people were finally realizing that their car was not just means to liberation but actually something of an encumbrance." "Once that gate goes up and the car comes in, people apparently enter this no-man's-land, a place where civic order and rules cease to apply. People lose a sense of perspective and self and feel very entitled to park."

In another segment the attendants reflect on how cars have grown in size over the years, to a point where they had to turn customers away because their vehicles were too big. "You could almost see the truncated syllogism in their head," one attendant says. "Like: 'I bought the car; how could there not be a place to park it? Surely it comes with a parking space.'"

Insurance companies, fast food companies, and car manufacturers have often used this parking lot behavior as a metaphor for selling their products. In 2007, for example, a Kia Motors commercial addresses the finding of a precious parking spot by using the childhood game musical chairs as a metaphor. In the commercial, cars slowly drive in a circle around parking spots while music plays, and when it stops, all the cars rush into the parking spaces. As in musical chairs, there is one more car than parking spaces. The extra car drives away after all the spots are taken. The music starts back up and the cars then pull out and begin driving in a circle again.

NATURE

ENVIRONMENTAL COSTS
One of the drastic changes caused by development is its effect on soils, vegetation, and water. Obviously, with the increase of impervious surfaces, stormwater volume and speed increase. A one-acre parking lot produces almost 16 times the volume of runoff as that from a similarly sized meadow; it not only increases water volume runoff but also prevents recharge of the aquifer. When increased volumes of surface water reach existing streams, the shape of the stream channel deteriorates rapidly. Streams in such urbanized areas often lose their ragged vegetated edges, small natural pools and woody debris, resulting in a margin of stones and wide washes. As runoff flows across paved parking lots, water temperature rises and pollutants such as oil, metals, and soils are carried into streams and waterways. Consequently, decreases in oxygen levels and increases in nitrogen threaten the thresholds needed to keep a healthy habitat.

Excessive impervious surfaces and piped drainage systems associated with parking lot design also pose a danger to the supply of potable water. A joint study by the American Rivers, the Natural Resources Defense Council, and Smart Growth America showed that in some of the largest metropolitan areas, the potential amount of water not infiltrated annually ranges from 14.4 billion gallons in Dallas to 132.8 billion gallons in Atlanta. Atlanta's "losses" in 1997, for example, amount to enough water to supply the average daily household needs of 1.5 million to 3.6 million people per year.[49]

ENERGY COSTS
Environmental impacts of parking are not limited to water, heat, increases of impervious surfaces or decreases in natural habitat. Parking also has a drastic bearing on the energy and emission contributions from vehicles. In a research paper titled "Parking Infrastructure: Energy, Emissions, and Automobile Life-Cycle Environmental Accounting," Mikhail Chester, Arpad Horvath, and Samer Madanat calculated the life-cycle environmental cost of construction, use, and maintenance of parking spaces in the United States. By adding their estimates to the emissions caused by an average vehicle over its lifetime, they showed that parking spaces raise:

· The amount of carbon dioxide emitted per mile by as much as 10 percent for an average car.
· The amount of other gases such as sulfur by as much as 25 percent and the amount of soot by as much as 90 percent.[50]

PARKED WATER

Most parking lots are paved with watertight concrete and asphalt supported with water removal infrastructure. This engineered piping system is built in to remove water as fast as possible from the site to the nearest stream by a system of curbs, gutters, and pipes. Yet the consequence of efficiently and speedily removing rainwater has also caused downstream flooding, erosion, and loss of valuable property and land. Calls for amending drainage practices had their influence in the 1970s with the establishment of ordinances for on-site water detention. The idea was a simple one: hold the extra surface water generated by development, and release it after the storm was over. This was most commonly implemented through the design of detention ponds.

Systems of ponds sprouted all over the country. Hoping to mitigate the ever-increasing developments with their impervious surfaces, localities demanded, through rules and regulations, the construction of detention systems. Yet as more of these ponds were constructed, more flooding continued to happen—except, flooding lasted longer or peaked well after the storm was over. Furthermore, these ordinances have more often than not created ugly depressions lined with rocks and invasive grasses. As many of these ponds are located in parking lots near residential structures, a detention pond designed to store water temporarily had to be entirely fenced with a barrier at least 5 feet high.

Stormwater runoff problems are exacerbated when parking lots are laid out as a large contiguous surface. Add to this wide and long parking stalls, large access ways for maneuvering, and lack of medians, and the result is extensive paving and increased water runoff.

LOTS OF HEAT

With the replacement of natural vegetated surfaces with rooftops, streets and parking lots composed of asphalt and concrete, overall city temperatures are on the rise. The temperatures of these artificial surfaces can be 68 to 104°F (20 to 40°C) higher than vegetated surfaces. Asphalt pavement, in particular, accumulates excessive heat because of its dark color and low moisture content. Pavement acts as a "thermal battery"; heat collects during the day and is released slowly overnight. This produces a dome of elevated warmer air temperatures ("urban heat island") over the city, compared to the air temperatures over adjacent rural areas.

A remote sensing experiment by the National Aeronautics and Space Administration (NASA) of scanned temperatures in Huntsville, Alabama showed that heating of road and parking lot surfaces, especially those using asphalt, contributed most to warming patterns. In specific measurements of a mall and its surrounding parking lot, an average temperature of 113°F (45°C) was recorded compared with a nearby forested area at 85°F (29.6°C). In a spot check, day temperatures in the middle of the parking lot reached about 120°F (48.8°C). However, a small tree island planter containing a couple of trees in the parking lot reduced the temperature by almost 30°F (17.2°C).[51]

BRIGHT LOTS

A glowing parking lot, radiating obtrusive light into the night sky, is a common spectacle of poor engineering. Ill-designed lighting tends to wash out the darkness low in the sky and trespass onto adjacent properties. Badly designed, polluting illumination does not only cause glare and harsh shadows but also generates higher than normal operating costs. In fact, more glare does not mean more light. Glaring parking lots are an indicator of inefficient and ineffective illumination.

To reduce light pollution, some communities have been adopting outdoor lighting bylaws requiring specifications for anti-glare and no-spill-off measures. Selection of the correct luminaire optics,

1.24
Las Vegas, Nevada. The temperatures of asphalt surfaces can be 68 to 104°F (20 to 40°C) higher than vegetated surfaces. Bare parking lots, in particular, accumulate excessive heat because of the asphalt's dark color and low moisture content. © Karyn Hinkle

1.25
Badly designed, polluting lot lighting not only
causes glare and harsh shadows but also
generates higher than normal operating costs.
© Colin Rosenow

the correct pole placement layout and appropriate pole height, and requiring shielding accessories all help to reduce light pollution.

LANDSCAPE

Parking landscaping ordinances emerged in the mid-twentieth century as a response to the unsightly appearance of surface lots. In later years codes were adjusted to address environmental concerns such as shading and stormwater runoff, although in many instances they remained aesthetically centered. Reviews of such regulations across various municipalities show similarities in both their intent and their purpose. Clauses often describe regulatory purposes as: beautification and visual quality, mitigation of annoyances, and environmental benefits.[52] San Francisco Green Landscaping Ordinance, for example, states the following environmental and aesthetic goals:

A. Healthier and more plentiful plantings through screening, parking lot, and street tree controls;

B. Increased permeability through front yard and parking lot controls;

C. Encourage responsible water use through increasing "climate appropriate" plantings;

D. Improved screening by creating an ornamental fencing requirement and requiring screening for newly defined "vehicle use areas."[53]

Still, most landscape ordinances are minimal at best. Perimeter planting tends to be the most common requirement. Perimeter plantings serve the dual purpose of screening what is often considered an unsightly parking lot, and buffering between incompatible land uses, such as commercial parking and adjacent residential housing. Perimeter planting has fairly weak environmental benefits because little pavement is shaded, and such planting may become less important over time as communities shift to mixed-use urban development and parking lots become integrated into their surroundings.

Regulations for landscaping in the interior of lots vary as to goals and purpose. Most communities do not require landscape improvements for lots with fewer than 20 parking spaces. Examples with lower minimums include: Colorado Springs, Colorado at 15 spaces; Salisbury, North Carolina at 12 spaces; and Virginia Beach, Virginia at 10 spaces.[54] Originally intended as a mechanism to control traffic routing and guidance more than for shading, coverage of tree canopy over paved surfaces was often ignored. Requirements tend to demand a certain percentage of landscaped area as a ratio to the total paved surface (generally ranging from 2 to 10 percent landscaped lot coverage), but do not specify the location or distribution of planting. Because developers often comply by pushing landscaping to the perimeters, some communities have started specifying actual canopy coverage to ensure distribution of trees throughout the lot. Portland, Oregon, for example, requires "one large tree per 4 parking spaces, one medium tree per 3 parking spaces, or one small tree per 2 parking spaces. At least 20 percent of trees must be evergreen."[55] Sacramento, California has one of the most complex shading requirement calculations to ensure proper coverage and to reach its stated goal of 50 percent shading of parking lot surface within 15 years. The amount of shade provided by a given tree is determined by using the calculation of the appropriate percentage and square footage of the tree crown as indicated on an approved shade tree list and a planting plan.[56]

FOUND SPACE—PUBLIC SPACE

In his book *Finding Lost Space: Theories of Urban Design*, Roger Trancik defines such places as "the undesirable urban areas that are in need of a redesign—antispaces, making no positive contribution to the surroundings or users. They are ill-defined, without measurable boundaries, and fail to connect elements in a coherent way." On the other hand, Trancik asserts, "they offer tremendous opportunities to the designer for urban redevelopment and creative infill and for rediscovering the many hidden resources in our cities."[57] Open, surface parking lots can be indeed considered urban lost space, but they are also an essential part of the built environment. They form part of a city's public realm by virtue of their physical openness and contrast to the city's architectural fabric.

The lot's distinctive spatial and use characteristics offer unique opportunities for their utilization beyond the temporary storage of cars. Indeed, from organized farmers' markets to spontaneous games of street hockey, cultural and social public activities in parking lots are a common occurrence. Such a range of activities suggests that parking lots, although not by intention, do form part of the public realm. Sociologist Lyn Lofland defines the public realm by focusing on its social aspects rather than its physical or statutory qualities. She clarifies: "You can begin to think of urban public space or the public realm as a kind of kingdom, one that is inhabited importantly, though not entirely, by persons who are unacquainted with one another: 'a world of strangers,' as it were. Like 'real' kingdoms, the public realm not only has geography, it has history, culture (behavioral norms, aesthetic values, preferred pleasures), and a complex web of internal relationships."[58]

Parking lots, with their intended and unintended usages, are a found place. They are the unplanned urban rooms that fill physical and mental gaps in our designed environment. Places where counter-interactions and social occurrences are happening on a daily basis.

FLOWER CORNER

For over thirty years a small corner of a parking lot in Somerville, Massachusetts, has been occupied by a truck flower "shop." It occupies a corner of the lot—an otherwise unusable space due to the lot geometry—yet in clear view of the adjacent busy street intersection. The flowers are placed on boxes that line the sidewalk, giving an edge and definition to the street and the parking. When asked if lower overhead cost had anything to do with the longevity of a business set in a parking lot, a man working there replied that it is "all about location."[59]

1.26

Many parking ordinances do not include landscape requirements. Those that do often tend to be minimal, stipulating exterior screening or demarcation. Lately, with growing concerns over environmental impacts, some regulations have started to stipulate better shade coverage and precise planting plan approval. Courtesy Denver Public Library

1.27

A flower shop at the corner of a supermarket parking lot. © Kathy Ziegenfuss

1.28
Underutilized lots turn into busy colorful markets,
where farmers, professional vendors, or just
any person can sell, barter, or buy goods. Every
Saturday, the Maasai tribe of Kenya holds a market at
the parking lot near the Hilton in Nairobi. The tribe's
traditional scarves, embroidered shirts, woodcrafts,
and batiks are sold to tourists. © Brian McMorrow

SWAP OR SALE

From Nairobi, Kenya to Los Angeles, California, the scene is repeated every weekend. Underutilized parking lots turn into busy colorful markets, where farmers, professional vendors, or just any person sells, barters, or buys goods.

The Larchmont Farmers' Market in Los Angeles is located in a small city parking lot. Like many parking lot markets it relies on precise spatial and social organization. Temporary canopies define specific use areas, and walks and passages are clearly agreed upon. All setup infrastructure is provided by the vendors, while the organizer provides signs and elements to delineate the space of the market.

About 400 miles north of Los Angeles, the parking lot at the Ashby BART (Bay Area Rapid Transit) rail station in Berkeley is transformed into a large flea market. Every weekend for the past thirty-some years the lot has been used to exchange, buy, or sell used and new items. So entrenched is this custom within the public perception that attempts to change the use of the site have failed time and time again. The South Berkeley Neighborhood Development Corporation has for the last few years been planning to develop parts of the lot into residential buildings. Yet flea market organizers, with much public support, have opposed such development. As the warning on the market Web site states: "There is no alternative location that provides the same benefits, security, and central location in the community as the one the Flea Market currently occupies. Moving the Flea Market means killing it."[60]

Without parking lots many of these markets would not exist. Vendors, consumers, managers, peddlers, musicians and performers would have fewer options to interact and mingle. Paul Newly, a University of Southern California staff reporter, captures this unique space/place experience in the following description:

> Every Saturday, a small parking lot in Leimert Park Village transforms itself into a farmers' market. A handful of stalls are set up and people gather to have a good time under a big tent in the center . . . the music begins. It's usually jazz. And it's always terrific. The day I stumbled upon the market, there was a band of skilled musicians, along with a choir from a church in Inglewood. I'd gone to pick up a box of strawberries, but I ended up staying for two whole hours.
>
> It wasn't just the music. There was something there for everyone—stalls with tamales, bread, cheese, homemade hummus, brownies, fresh greens, and barbecued chicken . . . and even a face painter. The smoke from the barbecue mixed effortlessly with the music. . . . Everyone seemed to know everyone else. That's what gives Leimert Park its close-knit, homey feel. Before I knew it, two hours were gone, along with my strawberries, and my camera's memory was full. Certainly a day well spent.[61]

PLAY, DANCE, JOUST

Informal games such as street hockey or basketball are commonly played on parking lots' leveled asphalt. Basketball, in particular, has found a sharing ground within many lots. At Bentley University in Massachusetts, a large parking lot located within the sports complex is used for both basketball training and overflow parking. During the summer, with most students off campus, movable hoops are distributed, creating numerous playing courts for the school's famous basketball summer camp. The yard of St. Leo the Great elementary school in Oakland, California has basketball courts and various hopscotch games painted on its surface. It also has parking stall markings, because the school opens the space for parking on weekends for churchgoers. Similar arrangements are found at most of the other Catholic schools in Oakland, with the St. Augustine School even allowing parents to drop off and pick up their children by temporarily parking in the play yard on a daily basis.

1.29

Cologne, Germany. The parking lot provides a perfect stage for the Society for Creative Anachronism, as they practice medieval fighting techniques and exhibit cultural elements of the Middle Ages and the Renaissance. © Jerome Thoma

1.30

Marseille, France. Informal games such as basketball or street hockey are commonly played on the level surfaces of parking lots. Basketball, in particular, is found sharing space with lots around the world. © Parrot Pascal/Corbis Sygma

1.31

Somerville, Massachusetts. Movie on the lot. An outdoor movie showing as part of a cultural event. The screen and chairs make the space, while the lot and the building provide the backdrop. Courtesy Somerville Arts Council

1.32

Communal mailboxes may be designed as a requirement of mail delivery services, but their location in the parking lot (coupled with lot basketball hoops) can create a social convergence. Often sited at the edge of parking lots, such facilities in automobile-centered environments enrich, if only temporarily, neighborly contacts and sense of community. © Jing Zhang

If mainstream games are not enough, the parking lot at the Rockridge Bay Area Rapid Transit (BART) station, also in Oakland, California, provides a different training excitement. Located at the midpoint of a commercial district along College Avenue, the BART lot fills up every morning and clears up late in afternoon, like any typical commuter lot. Like other such lots, it is fairly empty during the weekends and in the evenings, and is therefore used for various activities from rollerblading to skateboarding, or even the occasional car detailing. However, each Thursday evening, the lot turns into a medieval battle scene. For over twenty years the Society for Creative Anachronism, an organization devoted to enhancing and exhibiting cultural elements of the Middle Ages and the Renaissance, comes to practice medieval fighting techniques. Using replica armor and weapons, the group has been transforming the parking lot into a large fighting field, with spectators and participants from all over the area. Both the BART management and its police view the Society's use of the lot positively. As a police officer remarked: "It allows the community to use the space that they might have to pay for somewhere else."[62]

MAIL LOT

In the early 1960s the Rouse Company was embarking on an ambitious project to create the new American town. The new city, to be named Columbia, was to be built on fourteen thousand acres in Howard County, Maryland. It would be complete with jobs, schools, shopping, medical services, and a range of housing types, all centered around independent neighborhoods. The planners of Columbia were specifically interested in using physical design elements such as narrow curvilinear street systems and extensive pedestrian/bicycle networks to enable the social interactions of residents.

One of their intriguing design interventions was to pioneer the use of community mailboxes for all areas, even in streets of single-family homes. The intent was not necessarily to assist the mail distribution, but rather to force neighbors to meet and interact with one another while performing a daily routine.[63]

While at present communal mailboxes may be constructed out of preference and convenience to mail delivery services, they do provide a social convergence regardless of their actual location. Often sited at the edge of parking lots or on suburban street corners, these facilities in automobile-centered environments enrich, if only somewhat, neighborly contacts and community sense.

BLESSED LOTS

For almost forty years, each summer through the Labor Day weekend, Reverend John Bowen, minister of congregational care, leads a Sunday drive-in service in the parking lot at the First Church in Albany, New York. While standing on his outdoor pulpit, Bowen surveys the 20-plus cars in front of him and delivers his sermon to the car-seated congregants. As the service concludes, several of the drive-in worshipers honk their horns in thanks.[64]

Drive-in churches have been part of the American scene for over half a century. By the mid-1960s there were more than 70 such parking lot places of worship across the country. Most famous of all was the Garden Grove Community "Walk-In, Drive-In" Church in southern California. Completed in 1961, it allowed Reverend Robert H. Schuller to push a button and raise two 25-foot-high sections of the building's glass wall, "leaving only open air between him and nearly 1,500 worshipers in 500 cars parked below him."[65]

Religious rituals in parking lots are not limited to organized congregations and established parishes. Every year in the days before the Day of Atonement (Yom Kippur), thousands of observant Jews gather in a parking lot near Jerusalem's main market to conduct the ritual of *Kapparot*. In this ancient ceremony, live chickens are whirled above the heads of the believers, symbolically transferring

1.33

The Garden Grove Community "Walk-In, Drive-In" Church in southern California allowed the Reverend Robert H. Schuller to raise two 25-foot-tall sections of the building's glass wall with the push of a button, leaving open air between the reverend and nearly 1,500 worshippers in 500 cars parked below.
© Robert J. Boser

1.34

El Mercado de Los Angeles, Boyle Heights, Los Angeles, California. The Mexican-American community's reverence and affection for Our Lady of Guadalupe (also known as the Virgin of Guadalupe) is expressed through hundreds of community icons, murals, and makeshift shrines. At least two such improvised sanctuaries reside within parking lots. © James Rojas

human sins to the fowl. In Los Angeles, the Mexican-American community's reverence and affection for Our Lady of Guadalupe (also known as the Virgin of Guadalupe) is expressed through hundreds of community icons, murals, and makeshift shrines. At least two such improvised sanctuaries reside within parking lots. The Self-Help Graphics & Art, Inc. is a community arts center in the eastern part of the city. Founded by local artists and a Franciscan nun committed to social change, the place has become an important arts and cultural center. In 1987, artist Eduardo Oropeza (1947–2003) began ornamenting the building's façade as well as a large statue of Our Lady of Guadalupe with ceramic pieces and mosaics. In 2010, the Los Angeles County Historical Landmarks and Records Commission voted unanimously to recommend landmark designation of the building to the State Historical Resources Commission, marking a the first step in the landmark designation process.[66]

The other shrine is located in El Mercado de Los Angeles in Boyle Heights. In the parking lot of this three-story building, which houses a Mexican food court, market, bakery, and restaurant, stands a mural of the Virgin. Engulfed by parked cars and framed by topiary, it has become a pilgrimage destination and photo-taking point for the market's many visitors.

MENTAL DOMINATION

MY TERRITORY
The parking lot is a place of psychological transformation. A study in the *Journal of Applied Social Psychology* highlights with statistics the antisocial behaviors people demonstrate in parking lots. It showed that drivers leaving a public parking space are territorial even when such behavior is contrary to their goal of leaving. Parked drivers took longer to leave when another car was present, and even longer when the intruder honked. Males left significantly sooner when intruded upon by a higher- rather than lower-status car, whereas females' departure times did not differ as a function of the status of the car.[67]

THE COW
What do cows and parking lots have in common? According to authors Leonard Scheff and Susan Edmiston, they are there to help us manage and diffuse our anger. In their book *The Cow in the Parking Lot: A Zen Approach to Overcoming Anger*, they suggest that anger and destructive emotions are best dissolved through imagined metaphors and allegories:

> You are at the grand opening of the new shopping mall on the edge of town. You've been driving around looking for a parking space for ten minutes. At last, right in front of you, a car pulls out of a spot. You hit your turn signal and wait as the car backs up. Suddenly, from the other direction, comes a Jeep that pulls into the space. Not only that, but when you honk, the driver gets out, smirks, and gives you the finger. Are you angry?

> Now change this scene ever so slightly. Instead of a brash Jeep driver, a cow walks into the space from the other direction and settles down in the middle of it. When you honk, she looks up and moos but doesn't budge.

> Are you angry?[68]

BALLET
Parking lots' stripes and markings are no more than a suggestion. It is common for drivers to ignore such markings while they drive through partly full parking lots. Often crisscrossing on top of the painted stall markings, drivers will shortcut through the lot to reach their destination. Collision avoidance and pedestrian evasion tend to result in an unorchestrated ballet of machines and people.

1.35

Congested parking, 1941. Courtesy United
States Farm Security Administration

1.36

© Stephen Kennedy. Source: Garnett
Shaffer and L. M. Anderson

Surprisingly, such driving behavior may even be safer than a regularly controlled environment. In the early 2000s, a Dutch traffic engineer, Hans Monderman, redesigned a streetscape in Drachten, Netherlands without any markings, and removed all traffic lights. In what is often called "controlled chaos," traffic accidents have declined and drivers behave more carefully than when traffic regulations and signals were in place.[69]

SAFETY AND BEAUTY

In the 1970s, architects, urban planners, and criminologists were interested in developing strategies to deter crime through environmental design. Known as "defensible space" and "crime prevention through environmental design" (CPTED), this approach is based on the theory that urban design and effective use of the built environment can deter crime and reduce the fear of crime. The three most common built environment strategies used by CPTED are based on promoting good behavior through designed elements. These include: access control (e.g., installing entry markers to indicate the identity of a place and to mark entrances), surveillance (e.g., placing parking lots in lines of sight of nearby homes and windows), and territorial reinforcement (e.g., locating shrubs and plantings to create semiprivate space in front of dwellings).[70]

CPTED strategies toward crime prevention and the increased perception of safety have also been applied to parking lot design. While one of the most common parking lot design approaches is to maintain vistas and reduce vegetation (natural surveillance), research also shows that feeling secure in parking lots correlates with attractive landscaping. The research suggests that vegetation may increase perceptions of both attractiveness and security if it is well maintained and attractively landscaped. The presence of unmaintained, weedy vegetation might have the opposite effect on security perceptions, particularly in isolated, rundown areas.[71] Interestingly, the researchers found that perceptions of the security and attractiveness of any given parking lot were quite consistent throughout the group of respondents. While males reported slightly greater feelings of security across the board, the gender difference was minor. Such findings intuitively suggest that people assume if a place is looked after, they too will be looked after when in that place.

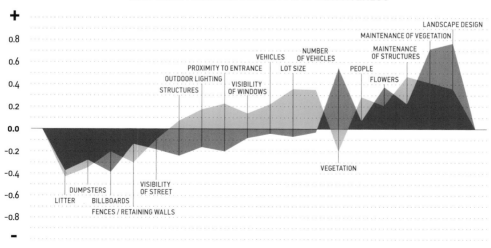

CORRELATION OF **PARKING LOT PHYSICAL FEATURES**
WITH THEIR PERCEIVED SECURITY & ATTRACTIVENESS

1.37

Front entrance to the Bullocks Wilshire landmark building, Los Angeles, California. The parking lot is the first—and the last—part of a space one visits. It is the gateway through which all dwellers, customers, visitors, or employees pass before they enter a building. Still, a site's parking lots are rarely, if ever, considered as an integral part of the spatial experience of a development. © Joshua Rand Kagan

1.38

Resort hotel, French West Indies. Resorts are one of the few types of development that place attention on the siting and design of parking lots as part of the overall sequential arrival and departure experience. © Charles Brewer

FIRST AND LAST

Too many designers and architects approach building design as the creation of a discrete object, neutral to its surroundings, and arbitrarily placed in the landscape. Adjacent parking lots are rarely, if ever, considered as an integral part of the spatial experience of development. Still, the parking lot is the first—and the last—part of a space one visits or lives next to. It is the gateway through which all dwellers, customers, visitors, or employees pass before they enter a building. Architects and designers often discuss the importance of the approach as setting the tone for a place, as the setting for the architecture itself. Developers talk about the importance of "first impressions" to the overall atmosphere conveyed to the user. Yet, with the prevailing ambivalence toward cars, and the refusal to view them as possible design elements, vehicles and parking lots are dealt with as a necessary evil.

RESORTS ONLY

Resorts are one of the few types of development that do pay attention to the siting and design of parking lots as part of the overall sequential arrival and departure experience. Sensibly enough, scenic hotels focus on creating memorable experiences in their surroundings that offer beauty, relaxation, and mental transformation. Such places would not consider having their guests enter the premises through a bare, paved parking lot with a shimmering sea of cars. Most see the parking area as a gateway, an entry by which a first—and lasting—impression is made. Whether employing ecological design principles or more common development practices, such destinations tend to carefully choose appropriate paving materials, and often incorporate existing features such as mature trees. By integrating these into the design, such resorts also place emphasis on the sequential movement of both drivers and pedestrians for walking to and from the parking lot, considering this sequence just as important as parking one's car in it.

1.39
Nantucket Island, Massachusetts. Groomed and
landscaped parking lot. Eran Ben-Joseph

2

LOTS OF TIME

2.1

Los Angeles, 1953: Control tower at new department
store, with electric signals directing shoppers
where to park. J. R. Eyerman // Time Life Pictures /
Getty Images ©

When were the first parking lots developed? Who was responsible for their design and planning? How have they evolved over time? What was their influence on cities, towns, and the built environment? In order to rethink and reassess the use and design of the lot, we should first consider these questions in a historical context. The inclusion of such historical-descriptive research is critical in understanding the impact of parking lots on design and planning decisions. By building upon this accumulated knowledge, further rigorous exploration can be undertaken and fundamental building blocks for new approaches can be set. Thus the aim of this part is threefold: to trace the emergence of the surface parking lot and log the chronological evolution of its design, to categorize the lot's morphology and style, and to map out the various codes and standards that shaped its form.

The historical query starts even before the automobile came onto the world scene. It begins with the management of ancient vehicles and their accommodating surface designs. The study continues with four periods that follow the invention of the car. First a shift from street curb parking to organized lots is observed. This reflects both the rapid increase in car ownership and the resulting problems associated with urban congestion. The shift also echoes the early twentieth century's enthrallment with rationality, order, and the scientific application of rules and codes to urban planning. By the mid-twentieth century, lot design corresponds to changes in urban dynamics, particularly growth of the suburbs and decline of city centers. The third period, around the last quarter of the twentieth century, is characterized by the utilitarian planning and design of parking lots. Universal application of parking lot criteria that disregard local conditions and discourage innovative design becomes the norm. The first decade of the twenty-first century is exemplified by a greater awareness of the environmental impacts of parking lots, and further incorporation of mitigation strategies.

BEFORE THE CAR

LET NO MAN DECREASE IT
Assyrian King Sennacherib, who ruled from 705 to 681 BC, had signs posted along the main highway of his capital city to ensure the route was kept clear of parked chariots. The markers read: "Royal Road—let no man decrease it." The king directed that any person whose property or possessions encroached upon the 78-foot-wide (24-meter-wide) roadway should be put to death and impaled upon a pole in front of his house.[1]

ROMAN PARKING
The act of parking or temporarily storing animals in the public right of way is as old as civilizations and cities. The earliest known rules for controlling parked vehicles date back to the Roman Empire. Around 2,000 years ago, the streets of Rome had become fetid and knotted with traffic. Local rulers became so fed up that they declared: "The circulation of the people should not be hindered by numerous litters and noisy chariots."[2] Around the same time, Julius Caesar introduced the first off-street parking laws. During his rule (49–44 BC) vehicles such as chariots and large carts were prohibited from entering the commercial district of large cities during certain hours because of congestion. Special zones (parks) were designated for storing these vehicles.[3] In AD 125, a limit was placed on

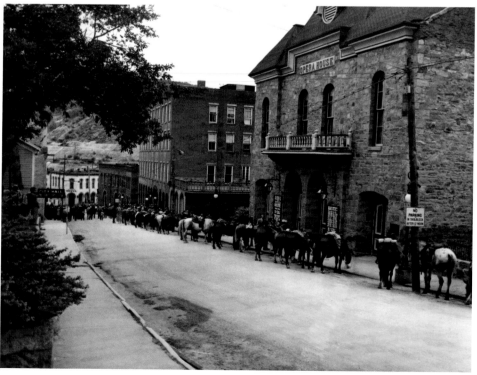

the number of vehicles that could enter Rome. It seems that as long as there have been roads, there have been multitudes of drivers searching for parking—followed by schemes for parking solutions.

ETYMOLOGY AS HISTORY

One might consider the use of the word "park" to create "parking" as some sort of an oddity. What is the connection between green, lush land covered with trees and the contemporary dreadfulness of a paved and rigidly striped asphalt lot? According to the *Oxford English Dictionary*, the word "park" was first used around the eleventh century to describe an "enclosed piece of ground, usually comprising woodland and pasture, attached to or surrounding a manor, castle, country house, etc., and used for recreation, and often for keeping deer, cattle, or sheep."[4] Its etymological roots are probably related to the postclassical Latin word *parricus* meaning "fence." It was around the 1600s that the noun meaning "a place to keep things" (such as animals in a pasture) was applied as a verb for keeping things in a place. About 200 years ago one finds the first suggestions of vehicular parking through the military usage of the word "parking" for the space set aside for artillery wagons in a military encampment. Finally, around the mid-nineteenth century, the word became widely used as a verb for stopping and leaving a cart, wagon, or vehicle temporarily.[5]

COURTING PARKING

With ever-increasing use of the motor vehicle, we find the emergence of related court cases and regulations. One such case is the early court decision of *New Orleans vs. Lenfant*, 126 La. 455, 52 So. 575 (1910), which defined parking as: "to bring together in a compact body, within a park or enclosure, objects not in actual service but held for use when required."[6] Many other court cases have dealt with regulating pedestrian and vehicle behaviors in the public realm. For example, in the 1800s, the Common Council of Indianapolis (Indiana) enacted traffic ordinances regulating drivers' behavior on the streets, but in 1915 the Council reflected the emerging dominance of the motor vehicle by passing General Ordinance 25, 1915, which regulated the behavior of *pedestrians*. The ordinance specified where and when pedestrians could cross the street, and also how they could cross it (not diagonally). This ordinance became a model that would be emulated by other jurisdictions around the country.[7]

CURB/PARK YOUR HORSE

In earlier times it was common for people who traveled by horse to simply tie their horse to a post, often provided at the fronts of buildings. This practice was known as "curbing" your horse. Almost all main streets of small towns in the United States had hitching posts for "parking" horses and wagons. Most streets were wide enough for "angled parking" for horses' carts and wagons.[8] However, in some of the largest cities congested streets and uncontrolled curbing prompted countervailing actions. For example, as early as 1690 New York City established a tow-away service in an effort to discourage people from "parking" their animals in the streets.[9]

2.2

Washington, DC, Arsenal Park of Artillery, 1862. Around the 1800s, one finds the first suggestions of vehicular parking through the military usage of the word "parking" for the space set aside for artillery wagons in a military encampment. Courtesy United States Library of Congress

2.3

Central City, Colorado. Almost all main streets of small towns in the United States had hitching posts for "parking" horses and wagons. This practice was known as "curbing" your horse. Courtesy Denver Public Library

CURB TO STABLE

Hitching horses and wagons to the curb continued until excessive amounts of manure produced at the curbing stations caused such a stink that it became standard practice to curb horses at the end of main streets in stables to contain the smell. Thus, the practice of clustering transport vehicles in storage was widely accepted and the roots of the modern clustered-parking lot were established. Later, motorized vehicles followed the same parking norms as horse-drawn carriages, and many of the livery stables became open parking lots and garages.

TREE PARKING

In the design of Washington, DC, the perpetual irony between parking of vehicles and use of the word park as a description of a lush green space got a new twist. Documents from the mid-1800s use the term "parking system" in relation to the creation of a park system, and the term "street parking" for the greening of avenues.

At the end of the Civil War a popular movement urged relocation of the capital to a more central location, spurred by Western land speculation, jealousy of the East's preponderant influence in national counsels, and the active promotion of journalists. As a countermeasure, in 1871, Congress decided to keep the capital in its current location, and to modernize the city by merging the jurisdictions of Washington City, Washington County, and Georgetown, and giving the newly unified District a territorial government.

With the consultation of prominent landscape architects of the time, including Frederick Law Olmsted, the city's civic areas were transformed by the addition of public spaces, paved streets, sewers, and the planting of tens of thousands of trees. Some documents suggest that Frederick Law Olmsted had proposed the term "parking-system" for the layout of broad streets with green, lush, parklike medians in the center.[10] In the proposal, the word "parking" is used in relation to street greening, specifically to describe not just medians, but the vegetated tree-lined strip along sidewalks. In 1871 the Board of Public Works established a "Parking Commission," with a mandate to "to report to the Board what trees they would recommend to the Board to be planted and the best places to procure them."[11] The Commission's actual jurisdictional status was not established until 1898, when Congress passed an Act "to vest in the commissioners of the District of Columbia control of street parking in said District," which stated: "That it shall not be lawful for any person to raise or lower the grade of any parking; or to pave or cover any portion thereof; or to construct any steps, walls, coping-fences, or other structures thereon; or to excavate or fill therein, except upon the written authority of the said Commissioners. These regulations shall not be so construed as to prevent the person having control of the premises abutting on the parking from sodding or beautifying the same with flowers."[12]

2.4

Laceyville, Pennsylvania. Most main streets were wide enough for "angled parking" for horses' carts and wagons. Courtesy Laceyville Historic Society

2.5

Pennsylvania Avenue, Washington, DC. Documents from the mid-1800s use the term "parking system" in relation to the creation of park systems, and the term "street parking" for the greening of avenues. Courtesy United States Library of Congress

Broken stones (Walnut size)

Stones laid edgewise

18.0

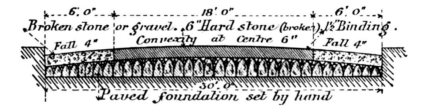

6' 0" 18' 0" 6' 0"

Broken stone or gravel. 6"Hard stone (broken) 1½"Binding.

Fall 4" Convexity at Centre 6" Fall 4"

30' 0"

Paved foundation set by hand

7.9 2 0 15.6 2 0 7 9

36 Roman feet

2.6

Top to bottom: Typical cross-sections of a French
road with crown, 1770s; an English road with
crown and curb area, 1820s; and a Roman road
(the Appian Way). © Aitken

Any discussion about parking must also cover the basic progression of road design and its technical development through time. One of the earliest known written laws, dating back to about 100 BC, fixed the width of Roman streets at a minimum of 15 feet (4.5 meters).[13] In Pompeii, up until 200 BC, the streets were possibly broad and paved with gravel and flat basalt stones, and the houses were low and small. From 200 BC to 100 BC the peristyle house with a portico became the fashion, causing an encroachment of houses onto the street and the formation of narrower arcade-covered sidewalks, similar to those in Hellenistic cities. This style was later adopted by the Romans and culminated during the imperial period. With the improvement of construction techniques, the Romans started to construct higher buildings that darkened the already narrow passages. As a result, Augustus (15 BC) limited the height of buildings to 66 feet (20 meters), or no more than six stories. He also made a new law fixing the *decumanus* (processional road) at 40 feet (12 meters) width, the *cardo* (main road) at 20 feet (6 meters) width, and the *vicinae* (side road) at 15 feet (4.5 meters) width.[14]

ROMAN CONSTRUCTION TECHNIQUES

Basalt slabs were the most common paving material within Rome, while the roads outside the city were either graveled or left unpaved. Sidewalks on both sides of the street were recommended, and often built. They were elevated, and took up as much as half of the street's total width. While basalt stone was commonly used in Rome for the road surface, Peperino volcanic stone, durable as the basalt but lighter in color, was used for the sidewalks; this custom was made law by Caesar.

By the peak of the Roman Empire, in AD 300, almost 53,000 miles (85,000 kilometers) of military roads (*viae militares*) had been built connecting Rome with the frontiers. The typical Roman road was constructed of four layers: flat stone, crushed stone, gravel, and coarse sand mixed with lime. On this surface, paving stones and a wearing surface of mortar and a flintlike lava were laid. By this time, the width of the road was usually about 35 feet (10.5 meters), with two central lanes 15.5 feet (4.7 meters) wide (for two directions) lined by freestanding curbstones 2 feet (0.6 meters) wide and 18 inches (46 centimeters) tall. On the outer side of the curbs, a one-way lane of about 7.5 feet (2.3 meters) was laid. This basic section and construction technique set the standard for road construction in Europe until the late eighteenth century.

STREET CROWN

It was not until the 1700s, with new light paving materials and new construction techniques, that street surface drainage was vastly improved. In 1716, Louis XIV of France formed the Corps des Ponts et Chaussées, a body of bridge and road experts and engineers, to supervise public works. This was the first body of civil engineers in Europe maintained by a government. An associated school (the first professional civil engineering school in Europe) was established in 1738. In 1764, Pierre-Marie-Jérôme Tresaguet, the head engineer for the board, developed a new type of relatively light road surface to replace the Roman cross-section that was still in use. His section was constructed with compacted broken fine stone on top of a square stone base. The roadway crown rose six inches and had a consistent cross-section of 18 feet (5.5 meters).

In 1765, London's Westminster Street improvement program created the first known "modern" city street section. Streets were lowered and leveled, and footpaths on each side were elevated, paved, and defined by curbstones. The carriageway was paved with smooth granite that sloped to small drainage channels on both sides of the curbs.[15]

In 1816 John Loudon McAdam, the general surveyor of Bristol, started a road-building program utilizing his design for a new surface. McAdam advocated the use of a well-drained, compacted subgrade soil that supported the load while the surface acted only as a wearing surface to shed water. His design consisted of an 18-foot (5.5-meter) crowned carriageway with 10 inches (25.5 centimeters) of surface material including 1.5 to 2.5 inches (3.8 to 6.35 centimeters) of stones laid in loose layers and compacted under traffic. His solution was widely accepted, and by 1820 more than 125,000 miles (more than 200,000 kilometers) of roads were surfaced using this method in England.

BICYCLES AND ROAD IMPROVEMENTS

From the middle of the nineteenth century, road development both in Europe and in the United States was held back by the expansion of the railroad. Although road-building technology experienced major developments during this period, vehicle performance lagged, largely due to governmental limitations on its development and a discriminatory policy that favored rail and stage coaching. Steam vehicles appeared in England as early as 1769 and were developed rapidly until 1866, when the Parliament passed the "Red Flag Law." This inhibiting ordinance required that all self-propelled vehicles on public roads must be limited to a maximum speed of four miles an hour, with a minimum of two people in the vehicle and a third on foot carrying a red flag to give warning and help control frightened horses.

The deteriorating state of the road systems came to the attention of the public with the introduction of a new and popular mode of travel—the bicycle. Invented in 1817, it enjoyed a peak of popularity in 1877 with the introduction of the low-wheeled, rear-wheel-driven "safety" bicycle. The bicycle captured the imagination of the people; it was cheap, safe, and offered convenience and mobility. The period between 1890 and 1895 was often referred to as the "Bicycle Craze Era" by newspapers and periodicals. As a result, both in England and in the United States, bicycle clubs such as the League of American Wheelmen constantly lobbied for road improvements. These efforts called forth local road-aid laws, enacted by New Jersey in 1891 and followed by the founding of the National League for Good Roads in 1892.

The public dissatisfaction with the condition of the roads fostered many complaints and petitions to Congress. One of the most impressive of these petitions, signed by thousands, including governors of many states, was presented in 1893. It requested the creation of "a Road Department, similar to the Agriculture Department, for the purpose of promoting knowledge in the art of constructing and maintaining roads."[16] As a result of this growing pressure, the federal government established the Office of Road Inquiry within the Department of Agriculture in 1894. For almost twenty years, the activities of the office were purely educational. It was only in 1913, after growing demands by motor vehicle users, and with the passing of the Post Office Appropriation Act, that the Office of Public Roads began engaging in road construction beyond that for experimental purposes.

2.7
Five Points, New York City, 1827. In the 1800s, streets
in America and Europe were dirty and unhealthy
places. Most were unpaved, and many had no sanitation
or drainage systems. Courtesy Valentine's Manual,
New York Public Library

STREET CURBS

In relation to street curb parking, it is interesting to note the historical evolution of the curb itself. Street curbs were first used as a way to control surface drainage. Evidence of such details can be found in archaeological excavations of Roman military encampments and in the design of cities such as Pompeii and Herculaneum. While including curbs as part of street construction almost disappears during the Middle Ages, when water ran in low street center channels and streets were primarily for pedestrians, paved streets with gutters and curbs regained momentum with the sanitary reforms of the mid- and late eighteenth century.

Curbs were formerly made of natural stone, but concrete curbs (typically constructed as one unit with the gutter) were increasingly used at the turn of the twentieth century—chiefly because of the decreased price of Portland cement. Yet it was still common practice to find natural stone, particularly granite, used for commercial streets where heavy-loaded vehicles frequently back up against the curb.[17]

The 1878 Roads and Bridges Act in the United Kingdom designated the curb as a lawful divider between uses. Subsequent court decisions against carriages using designated footpaths state that one cannot "unlawfully drive a horse, yoked to a spring van, being a carriage within the meaning of the said Acts, upon the loaning, being a footpath set apart for the use of foot-passengers on the south side of the highway."[18]

CITY HYGIENE AND THE HORSELESS AGE

Before the late 1800s, streets in both America and Europe were dirty and unhealthy places. Most were unpaved, and many had no sanitation or drainage systems. Even streets with good drainage turned to mud in rainstorms, and they teemed with effluents from horses, chamber pots, and household waste. The promise of the automobile was seen not only in terms of advancing mobility and commerce, but also as a way to advance health and the physical conditions of the built environment. An opinion piece written in 1902, titled "Some Advantages of the Automobile," claimed:

> The general introduction of the automobile in cities also carries with it numerous advantages to the general public. When the horse has become a rarity in city streets the wear of pavements will be enormously decreased, the dust nuisance will have been largely done away with, and it will be possible to keep the streets almost perfectly clean with very much less labor; the sanitary conditions of the cities will be improved and the noise and traffic lessened; owing to the greater speed and shorter length of the vehicles, there will be room for more traffic with less crowding, and finally, owing to the greatly superior control of motor vehicles, the streets will be safer for the pedestrian.[19]

FROM STREET TO LOT: CHAOS TO ORDER

By the first two decades of the twentieth century, "park" was widely used as the term both for a place and for the action of parking cars. Curb parking became a prominent traffic control problem and a topic of discussion among road engineers as well as public officials. Problems arose with more cars being added daily, truck loading and bus traffic increasing, and storeowners individually taking liberties to assign and construct curb cuts, all without parking sign regulations. But at the same time, controls and rules for driving and on-street parking started to appear. Some municipalities seriously considered banning all "pleasure" automobiles from city centers, while others entertained the option of eliminating all on-street parking, and allocating special lots and garages for temporary storage of cars. With the latter prevailing, municipal parking lots became one of the most dominant features of downtown America by the 1940s.

THE CHARIOTS THAT RAGE THE STREETS

Developed in Europe in the latter part of the nineteenth century, and introduced to the America soon after, the motor vehicle was still a rare sight on the streets of American cities in the early 1900s. At that time only 8,000 privately owned motor vehicles had been registered in the entire country, many of them propelled by steam.

The period from 1900 to 1929 saw the introduction of nearly 1,200 new automobile designs with various means of self-propulsion. This creative wave reached its peak in the year 1907, when 92 new entrants appeared on the landscape. In 1910, American factories made 181,000 passenger cars and 6,000 trucks and buses. In 1914, the production of motor vehicles exceeded the output of horse-drawn wagons. By 1939, 23 million vehicles were registered across the United States.

By the mid-twentieth century, the motor vehicle was in full control of the transportation scene, and has remained unchallenged since.

RULES OF THE ROAD

Up until 1900, traffic regulations were almost nonexistent in United States cities. The federal government had not initiated any regulations, and such traffic rules as existed were almost entirely the result of special legislation by municipalities.

Historians attribute the earliest recorded American law regulating speed on the roads to the Rhode Island Colonial Assembly, which in 1678 prohibited the riding of horses "at gallop or run speed" on the streets of Newport. Connecticut enacted the first automobile speed statute in 1901, and in 1907 the village of Glencoe, Illinois installed the first known speed bumps on its streets to discourage excessive speeding.[20] In New York City an assortment of ordinances scattered through its Penal Codes, Sanitary Codes, and City Charter attempted to regulate various driving behaviors. An 1885 city ordinance set a maximum speed for major streets, and other ordinances passed at intervals through 1903 regulated matters such as on which side vehicles should pass (on the left side) and on which side of the highway vehicles have the right of way (north- or southbound).[21]

THE FATHER OF PARKING RULES

Although he never learned to drive a car, William Phelps Eno (1858–1945) was a pioneer in traffic control and regulation. Eno is known for developing the original traffic plans for major cities including New York, London, and Paris, and is credited with helping to invent and popularize stop signs, taxi stands, pedestrian safety islands, and other traffic features commonly used throughout the world. His "Rules of the Road," adopted by New York City in 1909, became the world's first city traffic plan. He also wrote the first-ever manual of police traffic regulations. In 1921, Eno established the Eno Foundation for Highway Traffic Regulations, known today as the Eno Transportation Foundation, a nonprofit organization dedicated to studying and promoting transportation safety.[22]

NEW YORK, NEW YORK

It was not until 1903 that any serious attempt was made to apply compulsory rules to control street traffic in cities across the United States, with New York taking a leading role. The regulations were printed in small four-page folders for general distribution, and displayed on placards in public stables and along street fronts.[23]

During the First World War it became apparent that standard traffic and vehicle regulations needed to be implemented across the nation. As the war ended, the Highways Transport Committee of the Council of National Defense proceeded to test and revise the New York City regulations, with the objective of applying them throughout the United States. On May 8, 1919, the Council sought to promote a national standard by publishing as a Police Code the *General Highway Traffic Regulations with Safety Directions for Pedestrians*. By 1922, the Council of National Defense ceased to exist, and the legislation was transferred to the Bureau of Public Roads of the United States Department of Agriculture. With the help of the Eno Foundation, the Code was further amended, and received final approval and wide distribution in 1924.

Some of the notable articles of the Code included:

- Passing, Turning and Keeping Near Curb
- Right of Way Rules and Signals
- Ranking, Parking, Stopping, Following, Backing
- Overtaking Street Cars
- The Control, Treatment and Condition of Horses[24]

RANK AND PARK

In the early 1900s two words defined what is currently known as "parking" in the United States: "to rank" (ranking) and "to park" (parking). To rank was to stand vehicles (one behind the other) parallel to the curb (usually with little space in between). To park was to stand vehicles (parallel to one

2.8

Chicago, Illinois. Up until 1900, traffic regulations were almost nonexistent in United States cities. An 1885 New York City ordinance set a maximum speed for major streets, and other ordinances passed later regulated matters such as on which side vehicles should pass. © Underwood & Underwood / Corbis

2.9

Traffic control, Washington, DC, 1913. William Phelps
Eno (1858–1945) was a pioneer in traffic control and
regulation. His "Rules of the Road," adopted by New
York City in 1909, became the world's first city traffic
plan. Courtesy United States Library of Congress

another) at an angle to the curb.[25] "To rank" was derived from the term "cab rank," which was used in London, where cabs were positioned in taxi stands one behind the other in single file. The term "to park" originated from the practice of placing cannon carriages parallel to one another; in such a position these are said to be parked.[26]

DEAD OR ALIVE

Cars left unattended on streets or in public areas were a major problem for cities at the turn of the twentieth century. As traffic regulations evolved, codifying the use and control of parked cars was addressed by a clear designation of occupancy while the cars were "parking" or "ranking." Early codes suggest two definitions of automobile parking: "live" and "dead." A live vehicle is one whose driver is present and prepared to move the vehicle; a "dead" vehicle is one whose driver is absent or unable to move the vehicle. The issue of dead vehicles was seen as especially problematic at a time of no clearly designated parking and few ranked vehicles. During this time, chauffeured private cars were more prevalent than single-driver cars; this led to the theory that ranking could operate successfully only with live cars. Eno writes: "When vehicles are ranked, no one of them can move out of the line independently of the others, unless considerable waste space is allowed for between them, whereas when they are parked, being parallel to one another, any one of them can get away without causing any other one to move."[27]

PARKING AND CLASS

The inefficiency associated with parallel curb parking prompted two suggestions by traffic legislators: to restrict curb parking to live vehicles, and to allocate off-street spaces for dead vehicles. Eno remarks on the two options:

> The greatest opposition which we shall have to my recommendations (of limiting ranking) will be from owners of cars who have no chauffeurs, who will claim that class legislation is being proposed, whereas it is *they* who desire class legislation because what they want to do is to leave their cars where they will be a nuisance and a menace.

And he predicts the use and creation of parking lots:

> Vacant lots will be leased to store waiting vehicles and it will become profitable to construct public garages where cars can be left during the day when people are attending to their business and during the evening when they are at the theater. Some of these storage places will undoubtedly be in the congested parts of cities and others a little way out where people will leave their vehicles and proceed to their destination by street car, bus or taxi. This latter will be the case, I believe, in some of our congested cities such as New York where it does not really pay to go downtown in private cars.[28]

HOW LONG CAN I PARK HERE?

Legal determination of what parking means came about with courts' definition of "parked" versus "moving" cars. One of the earliest known rulings was the 1812 case of *Rex vs. Cross*, in England, in which the defendant was indicted for allowing his wagons to remain for too long on a public street. The court indicated that "Every unauthorized obstruction of a highway to the annoyance of the King's subject is a nuisance. The King's Highway is not to be used as a stable yard."[29]

CURB BLOWOUTS

A 1938 report by the Fisk Tire Company blamed 70 percent of tire failures on "one of the American driver's worst habits—jamming the tire against the curbstone through careless parking." The danger, this tire company declared, "lies in subsequent blowouts of damaged tires, which may wreck a car and result in personal injuries and death. Such careless parking may also knock front wheels out of alignment."[30]

THE DAWN AND DEMISE OF ANGLED PARKING

By the first decade of the twentieth century, angled parking was advocated as the best solution for parking and storing cars. This evolved naturally from the widespread tradition of curbing horses and wagons perpendicular to the curb; cars followed suit. With the growth of car ownership and the lack of ample space on main streets, angled parking was haphazardly introduced on narrow city streets to increase capacity. The result was often greater congestion, narrowing of driving lanes, and lack of passing space. Cars backing out of the angled parking also increased the hazards for passing cars. By the 1920s, a few cities had established specific dimensional standards. These included minimum street widths, travel lanes and stall (parking space) dimensions. In New York City, for example, measurements for angled parking stipulated that spaces should be at 90, 45, 37½, or 30 degrees to the curb, with an ideal width of not less than 7½ feet or more than 8½ feet wide and a length of 12 to 14 feet (3.6 to 4.3 meters) depending on the angle used.[31]

2.10

One of the American driver's worst habits was jamming the tire against the curbstone through careless parking. Courtesy United States Library of Congress

2.11 (following pages)

Chicago, 1930s. In the 1920s, cities across America started to allocate space for off-street parking lots. One of the earliest municipal lots was constructed in Los Angeles in 1922, followed by Flint, Michigan, in 1924, and Chicago and Boston in 1930. © Underwood & Underwood / Corbis

By the mid-1950s the striving for efficiency of traffic movement and the push for reducing points of conflict all but rendered angled parking a dangerous nuisance. Of particular concern were cars that parked front first toward the curb, and upon leaving backed out into oncoming traffic. Cities across the country outlawed its use and, with the surplus space, either added or widened existing travel lanes. Curb parking (ranked) replaced angled as the preferred solution of traffic engineers.

OFF-STREET LOTS

In the 1920s, cities across America started to allocate space for parking lots that were either owned and managed privately by commercial and retail associations, or owned by public entities and maintained by private operators. Some of these lots were within downtown areas, others were located at city perimeters. One of the earliest municipal lots was constructed in Los Angeles in 1922, followed by Flint, Michigan in1924, and Chicago and Boston in 1930. In Pittsburgh in 1927, periphery lots that could handle 900 cars, sited near the Allegheny River's edge, charged ten cents per car for those visiting or working downtown.[32]

In 1923 the National Conference of City Planning encouraged municipalities to take planned and rational action in allocating sites for off-street parking facilities.[33] One of the first comprehensive citywide parking plans was completed in Garden City, Long Island, in 1936. The first private facility organized, constructed, and managed by the local commerce association within a city center was in all likelihood built in Oakland, California, in 1929.[34]

PARKING SPACES WOMEN'S PLACES

Women's mobility at the beginning of the twentieth century was highly restricted, and their presence behind the wheel was considered "a step out of place." Yet, as women began to take an active role in shopping for their families, they entered the public realm en masse. This shift raised questions about "the value of women's time, the gendered dynamics of suburbanization, the right of women to enter public life, and the emergence of 'twenties consumerism out of an era of social reform."[35] According to some surveys of that time, California had taken the lead over all other states in the number of women drivers. In Los Angeles, San Francisco, and Oakland, 20 percent of all motorists were women. Women preferred personal automobiles because they offered greater flexibility, more comfortable conditions, and better opportunities for socializing with friends, and access for those who lived beyond the streetcar's reach.[36]

The rising conflict between women drivers, shopping, and parking can be illustrated by the parking ban attempt in Los Angeles. On April 10, 1920, the Los Angeles City Council decided that "since ninety percent of those who entered the downtown area did so by streetcar, the best solution to overcrowding on the streets was to ban private automobile parking downtown."[37] Almost immediately, downtown merchants were negatively affected by the ban. By the third day, "an advertising manager for Jacoby Brothers, a [major department] store in the area covered by the ban, reported that business was down 15 percent," reasoning that "there are many more women who use automobiles for shopping in Los Angeles than any other place in the country." And by the ninth day, "another merchant claimed downtown business was down 40 percent."[38]

The ban did not stop women drivers from getting their shopping done; they simply took their business elsewhere. A rumor in a *Los Angeles Record* article on April 20 reported that a woman drove with her car to Pasadena and bought $23,000 worth of furniture "because the police made her remove her car from the vicinity of Barker Bros. store a few days ago when she was inspecting goods there."[39] The result—the parking ban was overturned just 17 days after the regulation went into effect.

2.12

At the beginning of the twentieth century, about 20 percent of all motorists in California were women. Women preferred personal automobiles because they offered greater flexibility, more comfortable conditions, better opportunities for socializing with friends, and access for those who lived beyond the streetcar's reach. Women shoppers became a driving force behind stores' ample parking areas. Courtesy United States Library of Congress

2.13

In 1923, the J. C. Nichols Company constructed two 150-car-capacity lots next to the new Country Club Plaza Shopping Center in Kansas City, Missouri. Parking was free and the lots were beautifully designed with masonry walls, vines, flowers, trees, shrubs, and objects of art. Courtesy Kansas City Public Library

PARK WITH US—RIDE WITH US

Attempting to attract potential customers, some of the first private parking lots were constructed by street railway companies in the 1920s with the aim of providing ample parking space at their suburban terminals, making it an easy transfer from car to rail. "Park with Us and Ride with Us" was the slogan of the Philadelphia Rapid Transit Company, which established three large parking areas accommodating a total of 870 cars in different locales in the city. In 1927 they charged 25 cents per car, which included two round-trip rail tokens worth fifteen cents. No time limits were set, but an additional fee was charged if the car was left parked for more than twenty-four hours. Attendants were on duty day and night, and at two parking lots service facilities providing gas and oil were available.[40]

ATTENDING OR SELF-SERVE

Most parking lots in the 1920s were guarded and supervised. Actual parking was handled by attendants. They often required a large staging area near the entrance where customers left their cars. With mass popularization of the automobile, and the growing economic power of the middle class after the Second World War, customer self-parking became popular and eventually replaced the attended parking.

PARKING AT THE MALL

It is no surprise that some of the earliest surface parking lots in the United States were designed and built next to shopping centers. In 1923, the J. C. Nichols Company constructed two lots of 150-car capacity next to the new Country Club Plaza Shopping Center in Kansas City, Missouri. According to Davis K. Jackson, the engineer who worked on its creation, "This was a radical departure from the normal practice at that time, but it has since become widely accepted, and large free parking areas are generally considered essential for any suburban development."[41] Although Jackson advocated ample free parking, his actual design was sensitive to the overall site conditions. He believed in smaller, "well-located" lots, and emphasized that "it is important that parking lots not be too large." "Otherwise," he said, "there is a risk of serious interruption to the retail continuity of the shops." He describes the lot designs as "beautified . . . with masonry walls, vines, flowers, trees, shrubs, and objects of art." He endorsed the belief that such expense is justified as part of creating an attractive shopping experience.[42]

FROM CENTER TO EDGE: DECLINE AND GROWTH

By the mid-twentieth century, lot design corresponded to changes in urban dynamics, particularly the growth of the suburb and the decline of the city core. The booming growth of suburban development, and its associated auto-centric culture, spurred the decline of central business districts (CBDs) in many cities. This dynamic promoted the tearing-down of vacant buildings and their replacement with surface lots, in hopes of attracting suburbanites back into the city centers with "easy parking."

PROVIDE IT AND THEY WILL COME

At the beginning of the 1920s and 1930s, surface parking became an economic boon to property owners because good income could be generated without much investment in CBDs when depleted buildings were torn down.[43] At the same time, the process of clearing old buildings was systematically used as a form of cleansing downtowns of undesirable uses. It was argued that parking lots were the best solution as short-term profitable placeholders for depleted land while waiting for long-

2.14

Downtown Denver, Colorado. In the mid-twentieth century, downtown central business districts tried to compete with suburban shopping centers by tearing down dilapidated buildings and turning them into parking lots. It was argued that parking lots were the best solution for depleted land because they served as short-term profitable placeholders until the long-run prospects of economic recovery and rebuilding occurred. Courtesy Denver Public Library

run prospects of economic recovery and rebuilding. Studies from that period show the ample space provided. For example, a 1950s study by the National Parking Association showed that in the five largest cities one could find about 175,000 parking spaces in open lots in central business districts, with only 5 percent of those owned by municipalities. In Detroit's 1972 city plan, it was noted that "the automobile has an insatiable appetite for space"; at that point land devoted to vehicles occupied 74 percent of downtown.[44]

DESIGN ISSUES OF OPEN LOTS
Open lots, ready as they were for parking, challenged city planners. It was always assumed that vacant lots in CBDs were temporary, awaiting the next building surge. Because of this, property owners refused to invest in their lots as they anticipated a potential change in use, and city officials often agreed. This resulted in underdesigned and poorly maintained parking lots in CBDs, even when, as in many cases, these "temporary" lots remained for decades. This unfortunate situation set low standards for design and investment and a long-term acceptance of its default parking use by officials, users, and the public.

ZONING PARKING
By the third decade of the twentieth century, the first off-street parking requirements attached to new building construction and written into zoning regulations started to appear. A nationwide study carried out in 1947 by the Eno Foundation collected information from 586 municipalities on what types of zoning requirements they had.[45] The result showed that only 12 percent of these munici-palities (70 cities) had off-street parking provisions, and most were in cities with more than 100,000 residents. As can be expected, the study recommended an increase in legislation requiring a critical mass of off-street parking based on scientific measurements of parking demand.

The survey also offered some interesting benchmarks:

- 1923, Columbus, Ohio: The first parking ordinance with a provision for off-street parking in multifamily dwellings.
- 1931, Pueblo, Colorado: The first city to require commercial loading space off the street.
- 1939, Fresno, California: The first city to require parking provisions in association with uses other than residential.
- 1940, Detroit: The first city to require off-street parking spaces for theaters— one space per every ten seats.

Other noteworthy observations include:

- The most common ordinance for parking provisions dealt with multifamily dwellings, the specification of one parking space per residential unit being the most common requirement.
- Out of these seventy cities, thirty-one also had stipulations relating to the square foot area per vehicle. The most common was 200 square feet (18.5 square meters). The reasoning behind this requirement was the need to incorporate "ample room for maneuvering" into the specifications of each space, "since the land users, who in many cases do not have a clear understanding of the requirements of a vehicle . . . will, in all probability, allow an absolute minimum of space for such maneuvering."
- Forty-two cities had stipulations with respect to the location of a parking facility in relation to the building served. Of these, twenty-four required parking to be "on the same parcel of land as the building."

2.15
Early zoning of off-street parking requirements
provided an assurance of availability of parking
spaces. However, it did not address the design
quality of the lot. © Massachusetts Institute of
Technology, Courtesy of MIT Libraries, Rotch Visual
Collections; Photograph by Nishan Bichajian

- Regarding distances between parking and building served, almost 60 percent (24) of the municipalities required parking to be located on the same parcel of land as the building. The remaining cities allowed parking to be located at a distance of up to 1,500 feet (457 meters), with the average requirement being 275 feet (84 meters) between buildings served and parking.

The report concludes by stating: "The parking problem can be effectively tackled through zoning requirements. Sufficient experience has been gained to show that the requirement of off-street parking by zoning provides a uniform, impartial and effective means to improving terminal facilities in cities."[46]

DENVER VS. BUICK

Some developers objected to the newly established parking requirements and attempted to fight them on the grounds that they were unconstitutional taking. One of the earliest such battles transpired in Denver, Colorado. In 1956, the city passed an ordinance requiring landowners to provide off-street parking when new buildings were constructed, structural changes were proposed, or with a change to the existing use of their land. An automobile agency, Denver Buick Inc., challenged the validity of the parking requirement. In *Denver vs. Denver Buick Inc.* (1959), the Colorado Supreme Court held that "compulsory, involuntary off-street parking maintained at the expense of the property owner as a prerequisite to the exercise of his constitutional right to do business, is out of harmony with fundamental constitutional concepts." Although three justices dissented from the majority ruling, the court specifically stated that:

[t]he legal effect of the argument of the City is that it has a problem of concentration of traffic in the streets and that accordingly there is a right, under the zoning ordinance, to appropriate for off-street parking substantial portions of property of citizens desiring to use that property for a legitimate purpose, and to prohibit the use of that property for any purpose until its owners devote a substantial portion thereof to parking. . . . No such power exists in the city thus to take private property for a public purpose without compensation to the owner for the taking. It would be quite as proper to argue that the city had the right, under the guise of "zoning," to require dedication of private property for the street itself, if it were considered that a given street was generally inadequate to carry the traffic. . . . If it be true that a traffic problem exists, it cannot be legally solved by confiscation of private property without compensation, under a pretense of "zoning."[47]

While the Denver ruling was initially seen as a blow to municipal parking ordinances, other states immediately criticized the decision on legal grounds. In 1966, for example, the Massachusetts Supreme Judicial Court considered off-street parking provisions no more objectionable than requirements for fire escapes. It stated: "The reasonable premise of a requirement for off-street parking spaces for new buildings is that parking automobiles nearby is an established function of the use of any building wherein people live, work, study or congregate for other purposes. Such a requirement is analogous to the statutory requirements of public corridors and exits of certain size and number and somewhat analogous to requirements of fire walls, fire escapes and fireproof construction."[48]

With growing concerns over the environmental impact and the automobile's contribution to air pollution, other courts have continued to rebuff the Denver ruling. In 1975, the Colorado court finally overturned *Denver Buick*. As part of its argument it stated:

We therefore hold that off-street parking requirements are not per se unconstitutional as a taking of property without just compensation, expressly overruling Denver Buick on that point. We reach this conclusion with no reluctance. We take judicial notice that off-street parking is a fact of life and the fees generated therefrom by the owners are quite adequate albeit also inflationary. Studies of traffic problems uniformly find air pollution to be related to autoists moving slowly around block after block seeking a place to park. In these days of environmental concern, we cannot believe that it is unconstitutional to require those who invite large numbers of people to their establishments—who in turn clog the streets, air and ears of our citizens—to provide parking facilities so that automobiles may be placed in a stall and stilled.[49]

Today parking requirements are taken for granted. Even in cities like Houston, well known for its lack of traditional zoning, detailed off-street parking obligations are imposed on any new or modified construction.

2.16

In the 1940s, the United States Public Roads Administration advocated the creation of off-street parking for downtown area sites through the use of condemnation and eminent domain. As a result, cities like Auburn, New York, demolished large parts of their old downtown, replacing them with larger roads and parking facilities. Courtesy Bill Hecht

2.17

An ample supply of downtown parking lots in the 1950s provided a much-needed unstructured recreational open space for residents of Chinatown in Boston. © Chinese Historical Society of New England

2.18

The ugliness and visual blight of vast expanses of asphalt and acres of parked cars led to attempts to conceal their visual impact. In the 1950s, aesthetic considerations such as the screening of lots with fencing and perimeter landscaping started to appear in municipal regulations. Courtesy Kansas City Public Library

CONDEMN AND PARK

In the 1940s, the United States Public Roads Administration advocated the creation of off-street parking for sites acquired by condemnation. In a 1946 meeting of the American Society of Civil Engineers it was found that fifteen states had laws authorizing the use of condemned properties to create parking sites. Conversely, public officials branded traffic congestion in cities as a "malady menacing the cores of the cities and threatening the whole urban organism with irreparable economic losses through decentralization of business and industry."[50]

REVITALIZE DOWNTOWN

The 1940s saw a decline of tax revenues in American CBDs due to migration of businesses to the outskirts of towns into strip malls and business parks. Zoning for surface parking at the center of the city, and a greater involvement of local government in "solving the parking problem," was seen as a method to prevent decentralization. As stated by researchers at the Eno Foundation for Traffic and Highway Control: "Economic losses can be reduced by providing proper parking facilities for the central district."[51]

PARKING AUTHORITIES

While many cities solved off-street parking problems by enacting appropriate zoning requirements and forcing private developers to provide it, others saw the solution to be supplying it themselves. In the late 1940s, municipalities across the country were creating centrally located parking provisions through the establishment of parking authorities. (The first authority was established in Pennsylvania in 1947.) Created through states' mandates, these authorities were "special purpose public corporations, created for the administration of a community service of a public utility or near public utility nature. Although created by official government action, their activities are normally carried on outside of what is considered the governmental structure."[52] As such, parking authorities combined benefits (e.g., the power of eminent domain or police power) and responsibilities (e.g., fair pricing and a general duty to serve the public interest) to execute their mandate. Since they were also self-sustaining, they were protected from other municipal constraints.

With car-oriented shoppers deserting congested urban downtowns in favor of suburban malls that offered free parking, it is no surprise that the most urgent call for municipal involvement came from downtown merchants. While initially set to build and offer free or cheap parking on public land, most parking authorities were not concerned with increasing municipal revenues. Their aim was to reverse the downtown's decline in commerce, retail and business by offering low-cost, convenient parking. It was only in the late twentieth century, with the resurgence of the CBDs, that municipalities realized the potential for revenue associated with parking.

Even today, municipalities view the Parking Authorities as a crucial way to control their budgets and cover shortfalls. In 2008, for example, Chicago received $1.2 billion in upfront payments from private investors when it leased its parking system for 75 years.

The city of Miami, facing a $110 million budget gap, looked at its parking system as a potential source of revenue to replenish reserves and make bond payments. In 2010, a voter referendum proposed to give the city administration direct control of the Miami Parking Authority. The transfer of authority, the city manager claimed, would allow it to lease or sell parking assets and to issue bonds without the Board's approval, and to control the $2 million yearly contribution to the budget derived from the more than 30,000 city-owned parking spaces.[53] On November 2 the voters rejected this proposition, with the majority (56.5 percent) feeling that the Authority should remain as a semi-autonomous entity shielded from city politics and independent of constraints.

2.19

In the late 1940s, municipalities across the United States were creating centrally located parking supplies through the establishment of municipal parking authorities. © Massachusetts Institute of Technology, Courtesy of MIT Libraries, Rotch Visual Collections; Photograph by Nishan Bichajian

2.20

Artist's rendering of proposed shopping mall parking lot, Philadelphia. Design and aesthetic requirements for large shopping centers remain minimal. Most deal with tree planting within raised islands, the use of durable dustless paving surfaces, and the delineation of parking stalls by raised curbs. Courtesy Temple University Urban Archives

BEAUTY AND THE BEAST

In the 1950s, aesthetic considerations became an important part of the surface parking lot discussion, especially among traffic and road engineers. The ugliness and visual blight of vast expanses of asphalt and acres of parked cars led to attempts to conceal their impact.

Articles such as "Layout and Design of Parking Lots: Aesthetic Considerations," by Harold M. Lewis and C. Earl Morrow (1952), contained a good deal of information on beautification and aesthetic standards.[54] Artistry in the design of parking lots was appreciated by different groups—those using lots on a temporary basis such as shoppers, all-day parkers, and those living near lots. When considering the benefit of a well-designed parking lot for the whole community, the authors wrote: "It has been well established that a community with an attractive system of parking lots will attract retail establishments and office buildings. Such a community will also attract residents who find that they can shop conveniently in its business center. Each of these factors redounds to the great economic advantage of the entire community."[55]

The following general design principles incorporated in "the proposed new Zoning Resolution of New York City of 1950" constitute an example of aesthetic considerations of the time:

- Each car berth has a "free outlet" for exit all the time.
- Curbs separate parking berths from borders.
- Adequate drainage, with slopes of at least 0.5 percent and catch basins.
- One-way interior roadways provide circulation within the lot.
- Roadway widths: 16 feet (4.9 meters) for one-way diagonal parking, 20 feet (6 meters) for two-way diagonal; 20 feet (6 meters) for one-way back-in, 30 feet (9 meters) for two-way roads or any head-in parking.
- Importance of "protected walkways" for pedestrians in lots accommodating more than 150 cars.
- "Suitable islands" for ornamental plantings, trees, and lights.
- Dustless surface.
- In snowy climates space must be left for snow storage.
- Marginal strips should be from 4 feet (1.2 meters) up to 20 feet (6 meters) for trees and larger plantings.
- Lots located opposite residential areas should provide 15 feet (4.6 meters) of landscaped border.
- Walkways should be minimum 5.5 feet wide (1.7 meters), out of which 1.5 feet (0.5 meter) would be for bumper overhang.
- All walks should run "in the normal direction of travel," that is, toward the entrances of stores.[56]

PROGRESSIVE ORDERS

Considering the 1950s publication date, many of these zoning ordinances "assuring aesthetic characteristics" are forward-looking. It is unfortunate that since their thoughtful creation, many of them have not been implemented consistently. The following are some examples of zoning items dating back to the 1950s that deserve more widespread consideration and use even today:

- Importance of shade: "a canopy of trees at least partly covering the parking lot can reduce materially the discomfort to people if not actual damage to the cars."
- Mitigating impacts on adjacent buildings: When parking lots are located in the middle of blocks there has to be some means of mitigating the rear façades of buildings. Here again the ordinances advocate planting, "alone or in combination with a wall or fence."

- Landscaping: "Where walls are required as a border enclosure, it is usually desirable to supplement them with certain types of planting." In addition, this planting has a larger function, and that is to "unify the whole design" of the parking lot. "Where views of the outside are assets to the character of the lot the border planting can be less dense and even used to frame such views."
- Planting plan for each parking lot—a confluence of parking and park: The importance of choosing species that will be able to endure the harsh conditions of a parking lot is emphasized, avoiding those that require too much maintenance or interfere with other utilities (sewers and electrical cables).[57]

FROM ONE TO MANY: REGULATE OR NOT

Along with zoning and regulations for parking lots came the technological standards and geometrical configurations for their construction. With a focus on engineering precision and efficiency, cities and professionals shifted to an endorsement of quantity over quality. Gone were aesthetics as design considerations, replaced by a desire for excessive supply and ease of movement. The result has been an overwhelmed landscape filled with unattractive, harsh and unpleasant seas of asphalt parking.

STANDARD-SETTING ENGINEERS

The need for specialization in traffic engineering as a result of rapidly changing transportation issues prompted the formation of the transportation engineering profession in 1930, through the National Institute of Transportation Engineers (ITE) and a specialized education program at Yale University. The new profession was founded on: "A branch of engineering which is devoted to the study and improvement of the traffic performance of road networks and terminals. Its purpose is to achieve efficient, free, and rapid flow of traffic; yet, at the same time, to prevent traffic accidents and casualties. Its procedures are based on scientific and engineering disciplines. Its methods include regulation and control, on one hand, and planning and geometric design, on the other."[58] In 1939, ITE was approached for the first time by the federal government, the National Conservation Bureau, and the American Association of Highway Officials, and asked to suggest traffic engineering guidelines and standards in the form of a handbook and related technical publications. In 1941, the first Traffic Engineering Handbook was published, providing the basis for the profession and its practice. Out of 320 pages, only 9 were devoted to parking, with 3.5 pages discussing off-street parking. Little information is provided about the design of parking lots themselves. Most of the section is devoted to demand and supply, with design issues limited to stall geometry and dimensions, and location of exit and entry points in relation to streets.

Initial stall width and stall length recommended by ITE were based on a 1938 study by the Yale Bureau for Street Traffic Research. For 90-degree angled parking ITE recommended three options for stall width: 7.5 feet (2.3 meters), 8 feet (2.4 meters), and 8.5 feet (2.6 meters), with a consistent stall depth (length) of 17.4 feet (5.3 meters). The recommended backup space was 22 to 23 feet (6.7 to 7 meters). In a few subsequent editions of the book, the recommended dimensions increased. For example, the 1947 edition recommended a stall depth of 18 feet (5.5 meters) for 90-degree parking, while the stall width remained the same. By 1965, the third edition of the Handbook calls for minimum dimensions of an 8.5 feet (2.6 meters) width by an 18-foot (5.5 meters) length, "where skilled attendants park automobiles." However, in self-parking facilities, the minimum width was increased to 9.5 feet (2.9 meters) wide by 18 feet (5.5 meters) long, but as the Handbook stressed, "9.5 feet (2.9 meters) by 19 feet (5.8 meters) is preferred."[59]

STANDARD-SETTING MUNICIPALITIES AND ASSOCIATIONS

Some large cities, as well as interested contractors and transportation associations, also decided to enter the standard-setting world by forming committees to come up with parking design standards.

One of the earliest was the American Automobile Association. In 1946 the Association published *Parking Manual: How to Solve Community Parking Problems*. The *Manual*, the Association believed, would "stimulate greater interest in *action programs* for improving parking conditions both at the curb, and where more of them must be solved in the future, through off-street parking facilities."[60] In its text, the *Manual* covers a wide range of issues, from "cause and effects of parking difficulties" to "educating the public." Almost half of the book is devoted to a discussion on how to improve curb parking conditions and the planning and design of off-street parking facilities. Focusing on the central business district as the area with the greatest need for parking, the Association recommended three potential areas for parking locations: interiors of business blocks, fringe areas including those that can be served by public transport, and land owned by the city. As for the design of the lot, the *Manual* calls for the use of dustless surfaces with clearly marked stalls, perimeter fencing with suitable entrances and exits, and standardized stalls and backup dimensions. Landscaping or other aesthetic considerations are not mentioned. Parking at a 90-degree angle is highly recommended, as it "is the most economical of space because there is less waste space." As for the dimensions of the 90-degree stalls, the *Manual* recommends a single standard of 8 feet (2.4 meters) wide by 17 (5.1 meters) feet deep, with a 23 feet (7 meters) backup space.[61]

Another standard-setting association was the Parking and Highway Improvement Contractors Association. Organized in 1960, it "recognized the ever-growing need for more efficiently designed parking facilities and traffic control equipment throughout the country." It was "formed for the purpose of research and coordination of work to benefit its members and the public by producing standards and informational data and to assist in the development of codes and other pertinent documents issued by and relative to the industry."[62] A private/public-sector effort can be seen in the establishment of the Los Angeles Parking Standards Design Association. Formed in the early 1970s, the Committee was created to "provide the city of Los Angeles with the most objective, professional and up-to-date parking design guidelines that could be developed by technical specialists."[63]

THE MALL BUILDERS

The *Community Builders Handbook* first appeared in 1947 to provide guidance in the practice of planning and developing neighborhoods and shopping centers. Authored by the Urban Land Institute (ULI), an independent nonprofit research organization in the field of urban planning and land development, its major emphasis was to provide information to developers and homebuilders in the process of community development. For ULI, parking becomes a central issue when related to the development of shopping centers. "The space for parking customers' cars," ULI states, "is a basic requirement in shopping center site planning. After all, it was the automobile that brought about the still evolving planned shopping center. The layout of the parking space must assist in making the center serve its prime function—that of an attractive and profitable marketplace. In providing the indispensable parking, the only questions are how much area to provide and how best to arrange the space to be so laid out."[64] In its 1957 edition, ULI highly recommends a ratio of 10 parking spaces for every 1,000 square feet (93 square meters) of building area. This extensive and wasteful recommended ratio is backed by quotes from developers such as: "Our experience has shown that the smaller the center, the more parking space you should devote to it. You can't be overly generous." "In every business center we tackle, the headache is parking—insufficient parking."[65]

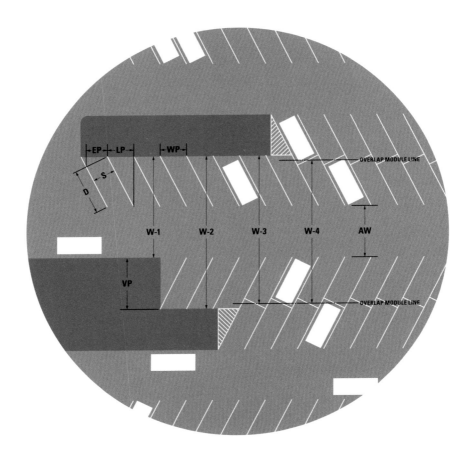

W-1   Width of parking bay (wall to wall), single-loaded aisle

W-2   Width of parking bay (wall to wall), double-loaded aisle

W-3   Width of parking bay (wall to overlap module line),
      double-loaded aisle

W-4   Width of parking bay (overlap module line to overlap module line),
      double-loaded aisle

AW   Aisle width

VP   Vehicle projection

SP   Stall projection

WP   Stall width projection

LP   Stall length projection

EP   End stall length projection

2.21
Parking design manuals have been primarily concerned
with stall dimensions, driveway widths, and parking
angles. Charts in these manuals show typical parking
layouts for various dimensions; they show that 90-degree-
angle stalls are the most efficient and economical,
with little "wasted space." © Stephen Kennedy

2.22

Parking standards such as those published by the
Institute of Transportation Engineers were devoted to
addressing demand and supply, with design guidance
limited to stall dimensions and geometry, and location
of exit and entry points. The resulting lots are oversized
and paved, with little attention paid to their visual
and ecological impact or the pedestrian experience.
Courtesy Walmart Corporate

While much of the extensive allocation of parking spaces has to do with the design for peak periods, especially during the holiday seasons, some developers' comments also reflect the bleak look of empty lots. "Don't design for the peak days," one commentator remarks. "The parking areas will have a forlorn look the rest of the time."[66] Fortunately, since the 1950s, the ULI research division has continuously reexamined its parking ratio suggestions and has adjusted them to reflect changing needs and times on the basis of actual survey data. In 1980 and subsequently in 1999, after conducting an extensive national study, ULI recommended a decrease in the ratio of parking to 4 spaces per 1,000 square feet (93 square meters) of gross leasable area, a major reduction in the allocation.[67]

DIMENSIONS—THE MATHEMATICAL FORMULA

Many individuals in the parking design field contend that optimal space usage, with proper parking and vehicular flow, can be achieved through the establishment of parking design standards as mathematical design equations. The engineering approach to a calculated stall design was introduced in a comprehensive study by Edmund R. Ricker in 1948 and published by the Eno Foundation.[68] Further engineering studies ensued. For example, in 1968 the city of Santa Barbara utilized a modified Ricker design equation to determine efficient parking requirements based on the angle of parking and stall width. The city of Los Angeles conducted the same study in 1971. In the report published by the city of Los Angeles, the authors state:

> The width for a parking stall is generally a resultant of the level of convenience provided the parking patron to enter and exit the vehicle in conjunction with the door opening movement. Observation, investigations, tests and experience show that a long-term parker is comfortable during the entry and exit movement from the vehicle with the 20 inches (51 cm) clearance allowance, while the short-term parker records 24 inches (61 cm) clearance. Based on a 6.6 feet (2 meters) wide design vehicle the recommended stall width is 8 feet and 4 inches (2.5 meters) for long-term parker and 8 feet and 8 inches (2.65 meters) for the short-term parker.[69]

In addition they suggest the following statement, to be included in any published standards:

> It should be noted that the parking standards are RECOMMENDED MINIMUM providing a comfortable level of convenience for parking patrons and vehicle movements. A higher level of convenience (generous) is obtained with wider stalls and/or aisles.[70]

2.23

Developers for shopping center lots tend to be more concerned with maintenance and operation of the space (such as snow storage and shopping cart distribution) than with the overall experience of the shopper in the lot. © Eran Ben-Joseph

PARKING AT ALL COST

The mid-twentieth century's preoccupation with driving and parking cars is reflected in two examples of successful parking lot construction by municipalities. In both cases the economic benefit derived from offering paid parking suppressed the previous use of the area. In Temple, Texas, a library occupying an entire block next to city hall was destroyed by fire. The site was used as a farmers' market temporarily, but in no time it was replaced by a 278-metered-space lot, which increased revenues for the city. In Quincy, Massachusetts, the city-owned marshland behind stores on the principal business street was filled and developed into a parking area with 560 spaces. As the authors indicated: "There was an immediate increase in business. Income from the meters totaled $51,000 in the first year of operation. Retail sales personnel and the sales volumes per square foot doubled."[71]

MOSES' LOT

Robert Moses, the power broker of New York City, builder of parks, pools, highways, and urban renewal housing, at one time had a good reputation. One of his first projects as Parks Commissioner was a revisioning of Central Park to include active play spaces for all ages, including sports fields and playgrounds. Starting in 1935, the parks department built 15 play areas on the perimeter of Central Park. Adventure Playground, at 68th Street and Central Park West, was one such playground that quickly became popular among the families of the Upper West Side. It was located just a short walk away from where the sheepfold that housed the Central Park flock was being converted into the restaurant Tavern on the Green. These two changes, a playground and a restaurant, fit into Moses' vision of a more active park, and coexisted peacefully for over twenty years. That all changed in a matter of hours in April 1956.

By the mid-1950s, the playground was frequented by middle-class mothers who came with their children to the play area on a daily basis. In 1956, the Tavern on the Green was a booming business, so much so that plans were made to expand the parking lot by an additional 80 spaces right over the playground Moses had built twenty years before. The Westsiders were thrown into a frenzy when one mother found a set of plans for the parking lot that had been left behind on a park bench. The neighborhood quickly mobilized to fight the parking lot expansion. Mere days after finding the plans, they submitted a petition to Moses' office. He promised a quick response, which arrived in the form of a bulldozer the following week. The mothers defended the playground with toddlers in tow, and managed to stop the bulldozer. They succeeded for almost a week in protecting their beloved playground, until 1:30 a.m. on Tuesday, April 24, when Moses demolished it under the cover of darkness.[72]

The "Battle of Central Park," as it was dubbed in the papers, was far from over. For three months it raged on in the press and in court, both sides trying to argue that their vision was more in line with what Olmsted and Vaux had wanted for the park. In the end, Moses surrendered and restored the playground to its original condition. The loss of the parking had no perceivable effect on the Tavern on the Green. For the next fifty years it continued to be one of the highest-grossing restaurants in the city. The restaurant closed in 2009 and its future is still undetermined, though it almost certainly will not include a parking lot.[73]

CITY ORDINANCES

Setting up regulations, ordinances, and approval processes for parking lots became a common procedure across major U.S. cities in the 1960s. While most addressed ingress, egress, stall dimensions and construction specifications, landscape features were barely mentioned and kept to a minimum. This was an unfortunate departure from the aesthetics approach taken for the design of parking suggested in the preceding decades. Although some exceptions, especially in private construction, can be found, most parking lot construction resorted to the bare minimum requirements.[74] Two ordinances illustrate the contrast between the positive stated objectives and the minimal stipulated requirements. For example, Chapter 38, 18.1 of the County of Fairfax, Virginia Code states:

> The objective of this provision is to protect and promote the public health, safety and general welfare by requiring the landscaping of parking lots which will serve to reduce wind and air turbulence, heat and noise, and the glare of automobile lights; to preserve underground water reservoirs and return participation to the groundwater strata; to act as a natural drainage system and ameliorate stormwater drainage problems; to reduce the level of carbon dioxide and return pure oxygen into the atmosphere; to prevent soil erosion; to provide shade; to conserve and stabilize property values and to otherwise facilitate the creation of convenient, attractive and harmonious community; to relieve the blighted periods of parking lots; and generally preserve a helpful and pleasant environment.[75]

Yet when it comes to actual specifications such as tree planting requirements, the Code is deficient and vague. For example, it stipulates that a minimum coverage of 6 percent of the interior of a parking lot shall be landscaped. Yet there is no mention of the type of planting, or if trees should even be included. Tree planting is mentioned only with regard to the perimeter or border areas of the parking lot, where the Code requires one tree per 50 feet of linear frontage, with an assumption that each tree will attain an average mature spread of 20 feet (6 meters).

In Culver City, California, a 1970 specification for the design improvement of all parking areas details paving standards, drainage, illumination, and maintenance. As for landscaping, a perimeter treatment is required with either an evergreen hedge or an ornamental fence. No trees are required. As for the lot's interior, the Code states: "large parking lots (of one acre or more in size) shall have planter areas provided at the ratio of one such area for every 50 parking spaces. Each planter area shall contain 100 square feet, and provide for one tree in an island with shrubs at the base."[76] Translating these requirements to an actual layout with parking stall dimensions and driving lanes implies that only parking lots with a minimum of 170 spaces require any tree planting, and in a one-acre lot with approximately 170 spaces, only three trees are required.

ACCESSIBILITY

With the rise of social and civil rights planning issues, design solutions to accommodate the development of accessibility criteria started to gain traction after the mid-1970s. As part of these efforts, Congressional committees and advisory groups such as the Building Research Advisory Board have showcased the lack of existing standards to accommodate the disabled in building construction and site development, as well as in parking lot design. It took another twenty years for the provisions to become law under the Americans with Disabilities Act (ADA) of 1990.

The handicapped parking space is actually one of the more visible and most successful accommodations of the ADA since its inception. In some ways one could argue that its sheer visibility and presence in every parking lot have made the disabled parking space, along with its adjoining iconic signage, the symbol of the ADA for most people.

CULT OF AUTOCRAZITY

In 1960, while addressing the Sixty-fifth Annual National Conference on Government of the National Municipal League, Victor Gruen, a noted architect and city planner, warned against the new attitudes by public officials whom he dubbed "autocrats." "Every attempt of those who believe in and fight for urban and public improvement," he said, "is brought to a standstill by the followers of a new cult which, instead of the golden calf, has chosen as its goddess the private automobile."

2.24
The handicapped parking space, with its iconic symbol, is one of the more visible and most successful accommodations of the American with Disabilities Act since its inception. © Eran Ben-Joseph

How deeply "autocrats" have been influencing the attitude toward city planning and development is characterized by Gruen's warning to the audience:

> How deeply autocrats believe in their dogma may be best illustrated by a statement in a report concerning the rebuilding of Los Angeles downtown, which reads, ". . . the pedestrian remains the largest single obstacle to free traffic movement." The cult of the autocrats, which I will name "autocrazity," is perfectly willing to sacrifice our cities on the altar of the new goddess. Their evangelists preach ceaselessly that everything must be done to facilitate and increase the flow of automobile traffic. Autocratic fanatics have already succeeded in leveling large parts of downtown cores of our cities, which now resemble the worst bombed-out European cities as they looked after the war. Some of our city cores, in fact, represent only tremendous parking lots and road accumulations, rendered inefficient by the few building which have resisted, for some inexplicable reason, the holocaust.[77]

Although the automobile remained a central part of life, its growing impact on the natural and built environment intensified the calls for a new environmental stance. By the 1970s newly established environmental organizations were calling for a renewed look at the way regions and neighborhoods were designed and planned. With the push for more walkable, mixed-use, compact neighborhoods, knit together by networks of transportation and environmental corridors, the generic approach to parking lot design had to be addressed as well.

FROM BLACK TO GREEN: ADAPT AND MITIGATE

In the 1960s and early 1970s, increases in air and water pollution, uncontrolled solid waste disposal, pesticide poisoning, and dwindling energy resources raised public awareness of environmental abuse and negligence. Books such as Rachel Carson's *Silent Spring* (1962) and Ian McHarg's *Design with Nature* (1969) set the stage for policy reforms and design measures. Regulatory mechanisms for controlling and reducing pollution resulted in sets of environmental acts and the formation of the United States Environmental Protection Agency (EPA). Urban design and site planning countered by integrating ecology and natural systems thinking into the planning process. A specialized field of environmental planning emerged within the planning profession which sought to combine scientific knowledge with design decisions. The result has been a slow shift toward a new planning approach, one that rejects the traditional binary view of human/nature to a synthesis of both in the creation of designed spaces.

ENVIRONMENTAL REGULATIONS

Ensuing public pressure resulted in government action and legislation to decrease and control contamination. The Clean Air Act of 1963, for example, was the first federal legislation regarding air pollution control. It established a federal program within the U.S. Public Health Service, and authorized research into techniques for monitoring contamination. In 1970 the Act was enhanced to authorize the development of comprehensive federal and state regulations to limit emissions from both stationary and mobile sources. To implement these new requirements, the EPA was created in 1971.

The EPA considered parking impacts to be as significant as other pollution sources. In 1973 it developed a traffic control strategy, known as indirect source review (ISR), for the purpose of reducing the adverse impact of automobile emissions. As part of the program, parking lots and terminal facilities had to be monitored and mitigated for pollutants just as were highways and major roads.[78] Complex analysis and impact controls were slowly put in place, dealing primarily with exhaust emissions and secondarily with other aspects such as noise level and drainage (stormwater) runoff.

The EPA did not initially regulate or encourage more integrated ecological approaches to the physical planning and design of parking lots. For its first three decades it concentrated on parking lot management practices and pollution control techniques. It was only in the late 1990s and the early 2000s that the Agency's publications started to assimilate and endorse new parking design techniques. These were associated with regional planning approaches such as "Smart Growth," water quality protection known as Best Management Practices (BMPs), and Low Impact Developments (LID). Publications such as *Our Built and Natural Environments* (2001) and *Protecting Water Resources with Smart Growth* (2004) stressed integrated techniques for reducing parking lot impacts as well as some rudimentary suggestion of design possibilities. Some of the topics discussed include:

- Encouraging mixed-use development
- Changing minimum parking requirements
- Encouraging alternative modes of transportation
- Minimizing the provision of parking areas
- Protecting and reducing water runoff
- Reducing disturbance and fragmentation of natural habitat
- Reducing of impervious surfaces

In 2006 and 2008 the EPA honed the emphasis on specific design solutions by publishing *Parking Spaces / Community Places: Finding the Balance through Smart Growth Solutions* and *Green Parking Lot Resource Guide*. While many of the topics covered in its publications remained the same, they also introduced specific design techniques (especially with regard to stormwater management) to include:

2.25

Environmental considerations in parking lot design include the reduction of impervious areas, the management and treatment of water runoff, and the utilization of landscape features. The parking lot at El Rio de Los Angeles State Park uses a native plant palette, infiltration areas, and permeable pavers. © Nitpicke

2.26

Reverse-angle parking has debuted in places like Syracuse, New York, and Seattle, Washington. With signage explaining how to park correctly, motorists pull past the desired space and then back into it. Courtesy City of Syracuse

- Paving surface and material alternatives
- Vegetated water channels instead of pipes
- Constructed wetlands in mitigating runoff
- Ecological infiltration systems
- Introduction of native plants

EXPERIMENT

In the early 1970s the EPA established a Technology Transfer Program aimed at funding demonstration projects to explore promising new techniques to control and combat pollution. In 1977 the Agency supported an experiment in building a new type of parking lot next to Walden Pond in Massachusetts. The intent was to create a low-impact paved surface next to a sensitive environmental area. Porous asphalt was pioneered as the main feature to combat stormwater runoff and explore its durability during the harsh winter season. Three decades later the lot is still in good shape and drains effectively.[79]

Unfortunately, and regardless of the measured success of this early experiment, the use of porous asphalt remains a novelty. Although other experimental and some commercial lots were constructed around the country (for example, at the University of Rhode Island in Kingston, and at the EPA's Region 2 laboratory in Edison), porous asphalt is yet to become a mainstream technique in parking lot construction around the country.

THE BOSTON FREEZE

As a result of the Clean Air Act, cities like Boston started to negotiate agreements with the EPA to reduce air pollution levels. In 1972 the Boston Air Pollution Control Commission, which was put in charge of implementing its agreement, included a freeze to the city's parking requirements. It allowed some limited exemptions (for example, for residential housing or hotels), but overall it was strictly enforced to cover all general public parking in the city. The result was that for twenty years (from 1977 to 1997), parking space area in Boston increased by only 9 percent: from approximately 51,000 to 59,000 spaces.[80] While the number of parking spaces was barely augmented, the cost of parking increased greatly, making Boston the third most expensive place to park in the United States. (The two most expensive locations were Midtown and Downtown Manhattan, respectively.)[81]

Although parking freezes seemed a fitting tool to combat air pollution, once other cities tried to follow Boston's lead, the U.S. Congress intervened. Trying to avoid conflicts between state and federal legislation, it forbade the EPA from reaching parking freeze agreements with cities. The decision to enact such regulation was placed solely in the hands of the local jurisdictions, eliminating any links between such bans and the Clean Air Act requirements.[82]

THE REBIRTH OF ANGLED PARKING

Recently, some cities are reintroducing angled parking with a twist. "Reverse-angle parking" has debuted in places like Syracuse, New York and Seattle, Washington. With signage explaining how to park correctly, motorists pull past the desired space and then back into it. It is a similar skill to parallel parking, but much easier since the reverse action is straight back, with bumper to curb. Such parking allows for more efficient space utilization and is considered safer since drivers exit the space headfirst, eliminating the visibility problems associated with backing out of the space into oncoming traffic of traditional angled parking. The spaces are also safer for bicyclists, since bike lanes would typically be in front of drivers as they pull out instead of at the back for traditional angled, or on the side for parallel parking.

THE PLACE OF NATURE IN THE CITY OF MAN

In 1964, landscape architect Ian McHarg painted a dreadful picture of what had replaced the pristine landscapes of yore: "Today, the modern metropolis covers thousands of square miles, much of the land is sterilized and waterproofed, the original animals have long gone, as have primeval plants, rivers are foul, the atmosphere is polluted, climate and microclimate have retrogressed to increased violence, a million acres of land are transformed annually from farm land to hot-dog stand, diner, gas station, rancher and split level, asphalt and concrete, billboards and sagging wire, parking lots and car cemeteries, yet slums accrue faster than new buildings, which seek to replace them."[83] McHarg's tone was urgent, and his assertions were provocative. However, his call, amid a period of awakening environmental consciousness, did not favor a return to the original, pristine state of nature. Rather, McHarg outlined a new "ecological" model of relationships. The basis of this approach was an understanding that humans and nature are linked through a complex set of interdependent connections that collectively form a dynamic system. This, he argued, was not merely a model of compassion or altruism, but a pragmatic step that was needed to establish a new way of designing our built environment.

Design is seldom practiced in a homogeneous space. Progressing from the specificity of the site to an idea, a program, and a plan requires a discursive process where boundaries are kept fluid. As we planners and designers enter the second decade of the twenty-first century, a new approach and different models may promise a renewed look at dealing with parking and the lot.

2.27

Women seeding a parking lot in Yunnan, China. Using reinforced turf or other porous surfaces in parking areas reduces heat and stormwater runoff while providing a green, soft background when not occupied by cars. © Carl L. Harstad

3

LOTS OF EXCELLENCE

———

3.1
Parking lot at the University of Copenhagen.
© Thomas Oles

Parking lots with or without parked vehicles can be fine spaces—even great places. Lots can be integrated into their surroundings with little or no environmental disruption. They can be social and cultural assets—a stage for open, less controlled behaviors where multiuse and multifunction can be achieved. Lots can be productive places that do environmental work—clean water runoff, generate oxygen, and produce energy. They can also be well designed with attention paid to details, materials, and architectural composition. The options are limitless. It is time to shift from modest and lackluster attitudes about parking lots toward attitudes that celebrate and acknowledge the great potential of these spaces.

INTEGRATION—IN

It is rare to find projects with fully integrated parking lots as part of their overall design scheme. Parking lots are seldom seen as essential to the arrival or departure sequence. They are not considered as part of the gateway experience, even though most people drive to and enter a housing development, a shopping center, or an office park through the lot. Parking lots are indeed the gateway by which a first and last impression is made. Yet every day hundreds of thousands of office workers, mall shoppers, and even museum visitors arrive at their destination by car, enter a typically bare and monotonous asphalted lot, park their cars, struggle to find a safe walking route, to finally arrive at a welcoming lobby.

Few designed projects take a different approach. In part 1 resorts are mentioned as one type of development that carefully designs parking lots to be part of the arrival experience. Some shopping malls such as the Tustin Market Place in Tustin, California and Bluewater Park Retail in Kent, United Kingdom have been designed as parking "orchards." Other unique examples will be mentioned in this section including the parking lots of the DIA Center for the Arts in Beacon, New York, Porter Square in Cambridge, Massachusetts, Solana Office Complex in Westlake, Texas, the multimodal rail terminus Hoenheim-Nord in Strasbourg, France, the Zénith Concert Hall in Limoges, France, and the old Lingotto Fiat factory in Turin, Italy.

DIA

The word *dia* in Greek means "through, between, across." It is also the word chosen by the Dia Art Foundation to suggest the institution's role in enabling visionary artistic projects that might not otherwise be realized because of their scale or ambition.[1] Part of Dia's mission is also the establishment and adaptation of existing buildings to show permanent and traveling exhibits. In 2003, Dia opened a major art museum in a former printing plant built in 1929 by Nabisco (National Biscuit Company) in Beacon, New York. The Dia: Beacon is sited on thirty-one acres on the banks of the Hudson River, and provides 240,000 square feet (22,296 square meters) of exhibition space, landscaped grounds, and an arrival garden parking lot.

For the design of the buildings and the grounds, Dia asked American artist Robert Irwin to work together with the architecture firm OpenOffice. The result is a sensitive composition of interior and exterior spaces. Irwin and OpenOffice, which specializes in the renovation of existing spaces, adapted the industrial building to fit the requirements for art installations. As the *New York Times* describes: "Irwin's modifications subtly enhance the viewpoint of the period. He has designed gardens in keeping with minimal art—and also with the simple, rectilinear logic of early-twentieth-century industrial architecture. Outside, there's a kind of grassy grid; hedge-like trees form straight lines. In the building itself, Irwin has inserted four clear glass panels into the structure's many large, multi-paned frosted windows. This creates a precise blurring of outside and inside, one that would be appreciated by the many Dia artists

who have worked with perceptual conundrums and by those—such as Robert Smithson and Michael Heizer—who have preferred to work with the landscape itself."[2]

Irwin and OpenOffice realized the importance of a developed entry experience to greet guests. They designed a site circulation sequence including an entry road, a parking lot, and an allée that leads to the museum's lobby. Taking advantage of the rising topography, the access road gently crests a hill, allowing a glimpse of the buildings set behind a geometrical grove of canopied trees. Once the road levels off on the upper ground plane, the actual parking spaces, defined by Cor-Ten steel planters and rows of trees, direct the guests to the museum. The parking arrival is aligned directly with the main access of the building entrance, allowing for clear visual clues. As one progresses from the slightly shaded parking lot toward the museum's doors, the final space of the sequence is an open grassy court flanked on both sides by evergreens.

Irwin and OpenOffice saw the parking lot functioning as the lobby to the museum, and intentionally executed its open and changing seasonal design for this use, while limiting the size of the interior lobby to a small room.[3] In paying close attention to the assimilation of the arrival by car to the site and architecture design, Dia: Beacon is a great example of how landscape, architecture, art, and parking can complement one another.

FIT FOR RECREATION

A 1965 report by the United States National Recreation and Park Association lamented: "Ironically, in attempting to make God's green acres accessible to seekers after outdoor recreation, we are inevitably forced to substitute large acres of parking pavement for that natural landscape which they are seeking. A family of four can sun itself in relative isolation on 150 square feet of beach; the car in which they came demands twice that area for parking and even more space is pre-empted by the access drives on which it arrives."[4] Parking lots in a natural setting deserve special consideration. Unlike in urban areas, they may need to be fitted into the landscape in an unobtrusive way, limiting their visual impacts and preserving the natural beauty.

Hengistbury Head, an attractive peninsula near Bournemouth, England, exemplifies such design. Since its designation as a public open space and recreation area in 1930, the 400-acre site (1.62 square kilometers) has seen a growing demand for recreational and nature-related educational activities. It is estimated that a million people visit the place annually. Complicating the situation is the ever-growing reliance of visitors on using private cars to reach the area. To accommodate the demand, the Bournemouth Borough Council constructed two large parking lots in the 1970s.[5] Trying to strike a balance among heavy use, visual impacts, and environmental pressures, the designers opted to excavate the lots a few feet below the existing grade. Using grassy banks and purposely not planting trees, which are uncommon in this windswept landscape, they totally screened parked cars from the approaching roads and the natural paths that crisscross the headland. Although the lots' design is not perfect (they are very large, and mostly composed of impervious surfaces), their siting and screening technique minimizes the visual impact of the vehicles while maintaining the undisturbed visual contiguity of the landscape.

3.2

The parking lot at the Dia art museum in Beacon, New York, was planned as an integral element of the architectural composition and the arrival experience of the visitor. Designed by artist Robert Irwin and the architecture firm OpenOffice, it is a great example of parking lot integration with its associated building.
© Richard Barnes; courtesy Dia Art Foundation

3.3

Aerial view of the Dia site. Michael Govan;
© Dia Art Foundation

3.4

Porter Square, Cambridge, Massachusetts. Artist
Toshihiro Katayama and the landscape architecture
firm Halvorson Design merged a typical shopping
parking lot with its adjacent busy arterial street
by treating the edge as shared space for cars and
pedestrians. Courtesy City of Cambridge

3.5

Toshihiro Katayama, view of the Porter Square
shopping center parking lot entry and exit areas
and the design's attention to the creation of a
distinct celebratory edge. © Eran Ben-Joseph

SQUARE AND PLAZA

Porter Square in Cambridge, Massachusetts, lies at a busy intersection of two avenues, a subway and commuter rail line, and a shopping mall, and has one of the few surface parking lots in the city. In spite of (and because of) this convergence of activity, the square was long dominated by cars, lacked a coherent visual form and a sense of place, and forced pedestrians to dodge traffic and maneuver through parked cars in the undefined parking lot.

In 1997, the city undertook a project to redesign the intersection and improve the streetscape. The centerpiece was to be new interface between the edge and entrances of the parking lot, the street, and the crosswalks leading to the rail station. Under the city's Percent for Art program, the Cambridge Arts Council commissioned artist Toshihiro Katayama and the landscape architecture firm Halvorson Design to develop a plan for the plaza at the parking lot's edge. The existing plaza consisted of three islands separated by roads; connecting the islands was the central design challenge. Katayama proposed a solution that drew inspiration from the preponderance of crosswalks in the area.

"To go from one island to the other, one had to walk on a pedestrian crosswalk. The crosswalk's black and white pattern was all over the place. I thought, 'I can incorporate the black and white stripes in my design to unite the three islands. Let's make a plaza full of pedestrian crosswalks!'"[6] Using large concrete paving blocks in white and dark gray, the design carries the crosswalk's characteristic stripe pattern across the entire width of the plaza, while a low steel wall and two freestanding panels extend the pattern vertically in key places. The result is a both a work of urban design and a piece of site-specific art.

Katayama conceived of the design as a counterpoint to the square's constant activity and movement. "I thought that Porter Square didn't need to be more colorful and complicated, because there were already so many people, cars, billboards, and traffic lights. . . . People wear red, blue, green, yellow clothes and walk in all directions on the plaza. I thought they would look beautiful if their background would be black and white."[7]

Beyond providing a place for passersby to sit and watch city life, the plaza mediates between the suburban-style parking lot and its urban surroundings, knitting the two disparate forms together in a harmonious fashion.

FLEXIBILITY = COMPLEXITY

Surface parking lots, with their relatively lenient regulatory constraints and minimal physical features, are spaces open to interpretation. Because of their less defined spatial context, parking lots offer a level of flexibility that can result in complex behaviors and uses.

In his essay "The Openness of Open Space," Kevin Lynch describes the inherent benefits of having uncontrolled flexible open spaces where even marginalized activity is accepted. On how to design and plan for such spaces, he writes: "One cannot rely solely on present patterns, since these are constantly shifting, and occur only within present possibilities and constraints . . . the designer's work is still incomplete, even if he provides a variety of facilities for a carefully analyzed range of new and existing activities. Since he is providing open space, his principal task remains: to devise forms which are uncommitted and plastic, which adapt themselves easily to a great variety of behaviors, and which provide neutral but suggestive material for spontaneous action."[8]

Parking lots may not be thought of as public open spaces like parks and plazas, but with their ability to accommodate the public and allow for both formal and informal uses, they should be.

From learning how to drive a car and ride a bike, to playing sports, or to just sitting in a vehicle and watching a sunset, parking lots may indeed be one of our most essential yet underappreciated and underutilized civic open spaces.

NAKED LOTS AND SHARED SPACES

An example of a flexible space that results in complex yet orderly behavior can be found in the "shared street" concept widely introduced in European cities over the past two decades. The concept incorporates the redesign of streets by removing physical boundaries and blurring distinctions between drivers and other uses. (This "naked" streetscape idea and its initial implementation in Drachten, Netherlands is discussed in part 1 under the heading "Ballet.")

The philosophical roots of removing boundaries and blurring distinctions between uses can be found in a report published by the Ministry of Transport in England in 1963. Authored by Colin Buchanan, a road engineer and architect, it sought to mitigate traffic impacts within residential neighborhoods. The report suggested a new approach to the management and design of these places through the creation of specific zones called environmental areas or urban rooms. These zones are of a different character from typical roads, and the level of traffic varies according to their function. Streets are evaluated not only for their capacity to carry traffic, but also for their environmental quality as measured by noise, pollution, social activity, pedestrianization, and visual aesthetics.[9]

This derived criterion—of environmental capacity—is then used in setting standards and regulations. Thus, certain environmental areas segregate traffic and pedestrians completely, while others have a mixture of pedestrians and vehicles. In the latter, vehicle speed and volume are reduced. The restriction allows pedestrians and vehicles to mix safely in the street, thereby reclaiming the social and physical public domain for pedestrians.

The Traffic in Towns report had a greater impact in mainland Europe than in England. German and Dutch planners adopted its tenets to such an extent that many still refer to Buchanan as the "father of traffic calming." Niek De Boer, Professor of Urban Planning at Delft University of Technology and an urban planner in the City of Emmen in the Netherlands, was inspired by Buchanan's theoretical ideas in his work on the physical design of streets. Trying to overcome the conflicts between children playing and car use, De Boer turned to Buchanan's concept of coexistence. He designed streets with such forms that motorists would feel as though they were driving in a "garden" setting, and so would be forced to take into consideration the other street users. De Boer renamed this type of street *Woonerf*, or "residential yard."[10] At the same time (1969), the Municipality of Delft was planning the redesign and upgrading of road surfaces in some inner-city locations. The planners decided to implement De Boer's ideas in working-class neighborhoods where more play areas were urgently needed but available sites were almost nonexistent. With resident participation, a fresh design was constructed to integrate sidewalks and roadways into one shared surface, thereby creating the impression of a "yard" and more play space.

The Delft redesign was a success.[11] Soon afterward, with avid lobbying by engineers and designers such as Hans Monderman, the "shared street" evolved into a "shared space" concept, one that not only dealt with streets but also encompassed all public spaces.

To achieve flexibility through design, shared space advocates stress the following observations and goals:

- Encourage sociable behavior by regulating less with signs and markings and by calling upon the self-regulating ability of people.
- Behavior in shared areas with a public character is influenced more by the expression of the environment than by the usual tools of the traffic profession.
- Let people negotiate the right of way and the vehicle speed will be reduced automatically.
- What feels safe is not necessarily safe. And conversely, what feels unsafe may actually be quite safe.

As the designers reason:

Better chaotic than pseudo-safe: Shared Space is successful because the perception of risk may be a means or even a prerequisite for increasing objective safety. Because when a situation feels unsafe, people are more alert and there are fewer accidents. Separating traffic flows often increases the feeling of safety, but in practice it appears to be counterproductive—the number of accidents with injuries increases. Separating traffic flows blinkers people and causes an increase in speed. Because everyone has their own lane, people take less account of other road users.[12]

3.6

Lennep, Germany. Shared spaces achieve flexibility by regulating less with signs and markings and by calling upon the self-adaptability of people and drivers.
© Wildfeuer

3.7

Redwood City, California. Shared spaces allow pedestrians and cars to negotiate the right of way. The result is predominantly a pedestrian place where vehicle speed is automatically reduced because of its multifunctionality.
© Eran Ben-Joseph

A LOT FOR KIDS

In the 1970s a few social reformers dared to challenge the typical use of inner-city parking lots. An article appearing in the *Nation's Business* provides an example: "Here's an easy, inexpensive way to cut down on costly vandalism, and help youngsters stay out of trouble: Turn over your parking lot to them after working hours." Citing examples from across the country, it showcased owners of parking lots who installed basketball hoops, striped the ground, and allowed local kids play after hours. In interviewing a local business owner in Jacksonville, Florida, the following story was told: "The youngsters in the neighborhood found out quickly enough what was going on, so we had no trouble getting enough of them interested. We turned over the balls to them and, in effect, the playground. We made it clear there would be no supervision. Nobody would tell them what to do or what not to do."[13]

NO STANDARDS

In the private development of Seaside, Florida, the residential streets consist of a uniform paved surface shared by pedestrians and cars. The design does not include raised sidewalks or curbs, and the narrow driveways and short street blocks control automobile speed. According to architect/planner Andres Duany, one of the designers of Seaside, his team avoided the restrictions of typical street regulations by labeling the residential streets as parking areas. Under this scheme, few streets were designated as major public throughways which adhered to common standards, while the rest were designated as parking areas. Labeling an automobile area as "parking" exempted it from typical street standards. The "parking" areas fell under requirements that were less stringent and more open to interpretation. For example, they did not require excessive setbacks for adjacent buildings, and driving lanes were not strictly enforced.[14]

3.8
Cape Girardeau, Missouri, 1960s. Teens enjoying
a summer dance in an empty parking lot.
© Ken Steinhoff

Surface parking lots can be a blank canvas for artistic expression and cultural statement. Whether as part of an urban palette or as an object in and of itself, the lot's surface and its transient nature can provide a unique opportunity within our built environment. Artists have realized the lot's qualities since as early as the 1950s—some have staged ephemeral installations, others have constructed commentary on social and cultural issues. Still, art in the lot is relatively scarce considering that lots are ideal places for both temporary and permanent installations.

THIRTYFOUR PARKING LOTS

One Sunday morning in 1967, the artist Ed Ruscha and a professional aerial photographer he had hired took flight over Los Angeles in a helicopter. The photographs they produced were published that year by Ruscha, in a book titled *Thirtyfour Parking Lots*. Starting with *Twentysix Gasoline Stations* in 1962, Ruscha produced several photographic series based on the idea of a typology. Around the same time, the German photographers Bernd and Hilla Becher were pioneering a similar approach, with their iconic pictures of water towers and other industrial structures. The typological approach was quasi-scientific; rather than seeking out a single iconic representative of a given form, it sought instead to create an index of all the variations in form, each one presented in an "objective" nonstylized format.

Many have interpreted the series as a trenchant critique of the southern California urban design paradigm and the landscapes produced by America's love affair with the car. Viewed within the larger context of Ruscha's work, however, this reading seems less plausible. It was not characteristic of Ruscha to offer such straightforward statements; his stance is that of the cool observer, one who sees but does not judge. His goal is to capture the sense of place, not to incite action. Indeed, he often seems to be celebrating (perhaps semi-ironically) the radical openness of Los Angeles.

3.9

Seaside, Florida. Labeling an automobile area as "parking" exempted it from typical street standards. Such areas fell under requirements that are less stringent and more open to interpretation, thus allowing for more innovative design solutions. © Peter Owens

Ruscha is interested in the ways that human tendencies are made visible in the built environment. In an interview, he commented: "Architects write me about the parking lots book because they are interested in seeing parking lot patterns and things like that. But those patterns and their abstract design quality mean nothing to me. I'll tell you what is more interesting: the oil droppings on the ground."[15]

THE STRAY CART

Cars and shopping carts—both have wheels and both require parking. Shopping carts bridge the gap between what a person can lift and what a car can hold. Stepping from his/her car, a customer makes a round trip—to the store and back again to the vehicle. But the cart comes along only for the return journey, often to be abandoned curbside when one drives off.

The fate of those carts left in parking lots (those that were not neatly returned to the cart corralling areas) is explored by artist Julian Montague in *The Stray Shopping Cart Project*. Using the language of scientific classification, Montague developed a system to describe the stray shopping carts he saw cluttering the landscape. The project began in Buffalo, New York, in 1999, when Montague began documenting stray shopping carts. Over six years he collected "specimens" (photos and documentation of stray carts) from Buffalo and other northeastern U.S. communities, continuously refining his classification scheme.

For example, Montague's first level of categorization divides "False Strays" from "True Strays." False strays are those carts that look lost but ultimately make their way back to their sources. Most do not make it out of the parking lot and are collected by teams of "source agents," usually employees sent on retrieving missions. "True Strays" never return to their intended use. Some true strays are taken over by individuals or businesses for other uses, and somehow find their way beyond two blocks from their source.[16]

3.10

Artist Julian Montague in his *Stray Shopping Cart Project* explores the fate of carts left in parking lots. Using the language of scientific classifications, Montague developed a system to describe abandoned carts he saw cluttering the landscape. © Julian Montague

3.11

When the architecture firm SITE was commissioned to design typical department store sites in the 1970s, they took an unconventional approach of joining interior with exterior. While the *Parking Lot Showroom* (1976) was the only site not built, it is one of the most provocative designs, with the parking lot rolling over the building. © SITE Inc.

GHOST LOT

Architecture is a medium of communication. This is the belief of the firm SITE, Sculpture in the Environment, founded in 1970 by James Wines to explore "new ways to bring a heightened level of communication and psychological content to buildings, interiors, and public spaces."[17] Over the last forty years SITE has executed over 150 projects, and continues to explore the theme of communication.

Their design process builds from the elements and ideas existing within the context of a project. Two of their most recognized projects have dealt with the relationship of the suburban strip mall and its parking lot: *Ghost Parking Lot* in Hamden, Connecticut and the unrealized *Parking Lot Showroom* from their BEST Products showroom series.

Ghost Parking Lot was commissioned in 1977 by David W. Bermant, President of National Shopping Centers, who placed more than fifty public art pieces in his twenty major strip mall centers around the United States. In this eerie monument to shopping trips past, twenty junk cars were buried in asphalt in the spaces at the street edge of the shopping center's extensive parking lot. The piece is at once familiar and foreign. The elements of the project—cars and asphalt—are commonplace, but their relationship is inverted. Paving holds these cars back rather than letting them access the open road.[18]

Parking Lot Showroom similarly shows an inversion. Here the store itself is subsumed by its parking lot. BEST Products, a defunct retail chain, commissioned nine showroom designs from SITE between 1972 and 1980. The *Parking Lot Showroom* (1976) was the only one not built; yet it is one of the most provocative designs. The parking lot rolls over the building, its stripes marked out across the entire roof, spaces that on the premier shopping day, Black Friday, might look enticing. In SITE's own commentary, "what is traditionally regarded as building and space-around-building would become integrated to a degree where it would no longer be possible to discern where one began and the other stopped—suggesting that architecture need not be an object distinctly identifiable as separate from its context."[19] This project celebrates the lot, suggesting that it is an integral part of a shopping center, not to be hidden, not to be looked past, but to be put on display. Its form can be read as a store rising out of its lot. The shopping center, in form and function, could not have been possible without the carrying capacity of a car and the expanses of paving that accommodate the shoppers' vehicles.

3.12

Ghost Parking Lot was designed and built by SITE in
1977 at a shopping plaza in Hamden, Connecticut.
In this monument to shopping trips past, twenty junk
cars are buried in asphalt at the street edge of the
shopping center's extensive parking lot. These projects
by SITE commemorate the integral part played by
parking lots in our daily life. Unfortunately, the *Ghost
Parking Lot* was demolished in 2003 due to poor
maintenance. © SITE Inc.

3.13

Transportation icons and symbols are celebrated
rather than camouflaged in this amusement center's
parking lot in southern California designed by
landscape architect Martha Schwartz. © Martha
Schwartz

PARKING ESPLANADE

When landscape architect Martha Schwartz was asked to design a tram drop-off parking lot at a theme park in southern California, she decided to emphasize the existing parking environment rather than camouflage it. Schwartz, known for her integration of art and landscape, used standard highway and infrastructural motifs such as traffic cones and crosswalk markings to combine utility with the playfulness associated with an amusement park. As visitors enter the area, the celebratory nature of the place—a parking lot with traffic, cars, and pedestrians—is vividly distinguished. The parking lot thus becomes a glorified place, not to be hidden but to be acknowledged and appreciated.

TERMINUS

As part of a program to reduce car trips in its downtown center, the city of Strasbourg, France developed a system of suburban park-and-ride lots connected to the city by a new tramline. Architect Zaha Hadid was commissioned to design one of these tram stations and an adjacent parking lot for 800 cars.

Seen from the above, the building and parking lot appear as a single composition, a broad streak of white on a field of dark gray. Upon closer inspection, one sees that the white streak is part building roof, and part parking lot surface. Because both are constructed in the same-colored material, there is a flattening effect: building and parking seem to merge together.

The design takes the essentially random geometry of the site as the starting point for an elaborate composition; the angles formed by the boundaries of the parcel are reflected back in the shape of the building, a jaunty, low-slung parallelogram. They also reverberate in the pattern of line markings on the lot's surface. Viewed in plan, the lines delineating the parking spaces appear to reorient themselves slightly with each successive row. At regular intervals, these lines peel off the surface and tilt upward, in the form of light "masts." As the site slopes downward toward one end, the light masts become taller. Although bare and without vegetated cover, the Car Park and Terminus in Hoenheim-Nord is a great example of integrated form and function; rail, parking, art, and architecture become one.

EVENT PLACE

In New York City, the Brooklyn Museum integrates open-house events with activities that spill outdoors during the summer. These large "First Saturdays" events often conclude with a party—complete with live music, food, and drink—taking place on the museum's parking lot. Not far from the museum, the UniverSoul Circus sets up its tent on the Woolman Rink parking lot. In Boston, the Cirque du Soleil takes over the old South Boston Port's parking lot for the show's duration. There is often no better staging place than the horizontal surfaces of a lot to attract festivals, markets, open theaters, or dance parties, formalized or spontaneous.

SHAKESPEARE'S LOT

In 1995, Jennifer Pias Spahr and her husband Robert were running a small off-off-Broadway theater company on the Lower East Side of Manhattan. While working on a new production of Shakespeare's *A Midsummer Night's Dream*, they chafed at the limitations of their theater space. "It's a very small theater, we would look out on this enormous parking lot across the street, and notice that it wasn't used at night," Spahr recalled. "It was an empty space. And I couldn't help think of Peter Brook's line that all empty spaces can be theaters."[20] Since the lot was owned by the city, the Department of Transportation told Spahr that in order to use the lot she must have the signatures of local residents on

3.14
Architect Zaha Hadid designed this intermodal transportation facility in Hoenheim, France. Building, rail tracks, buses, and parking for 800 cars appear as a single composition. © Julian Pierre

3.15
Members of Expanded Arts theater rehearse a scene from William Shakespeare's *Macbeth* in a parking lot on Manhattan's Lower East Side. Since 1995 the parking lot has been the stage for *Shakespeare in the Parking Lot*. Courtesy The Drilling Company

3.16
"What the Fluff?" event, Somerville, Massachusetts. A parking stall turned into a makeshift bowling alley furnished with convenient "bumpers." © Nobuko Ichikawa

3.17
The parking lot at Hotel San Jose in South Austin is converted into a concert and market area during the city's famous South by Southwest Music Conference and Festival (SXSW). © Bunkhouse Group

a petition stating that they agreed to the use of the space as an outdoor theater. As Spahr describes: "Almost nobody in the neighborhood spoke English, so I went to someone at the Baskin Robbins and had him translate the petition into Chinese." She then went around, stopping people on the street and getting more than 250 signatures.[21]

Between July and August, for the last sixteen years, *Shakespeare in the Parking Lot* has been drawing sometimes over 200 people a night while still providing some parking. When describing what draws people to this unique event, Hamilton Clancy, the current director, attributes it to the unique setting. There is something "so democratic about it, so unlike other theater experiences."[22]

PARKING FLUFF

One of the claims to fame of the city of Somerville, Massachusetts, is being the birthplace of Marshmallow Fluff. This sweet spreadable confection was invented at the beginning of the twentieth century by Archibald Query near the city's Union Square. In 2006 the city decided to celebrate annually all things marshmallow by declaring a "What the Fluff?" day. While some events take place in the small square, it is mainly the adjacent parking lot that is utilized for performances and a wide array of wacky games such as Fluff tug-o-war, Fluff lick-off, blind man's Fluff, and Fluff fear factor roulette.

SOUTH BY SAN JOSE

Austin, Texas, like many other smaller, vibrant cites located far away from large metropolitan areas, seeks to increase its attractiveness to outsiders. One successful method of doing so is to create conferences, and sports or cultural gatherings that attract visitors from all over the country. The South by Southwest Music Conference and Festival (SXSW) is intended to do just that. Inaugurated in 1987, the festival brings to a concentrated area in the city an eclectic collection of country, folk, jazz, blues, and rock music. Although it is mainly held at indoor venues, some local establishments have seized the opportunity to offer their own free venues and attract an out-of-town clientele. One example of this is the Hotel San Jose in South Austin. During the festival it converts its parking lot into an event space, set up with a temporary stage and performers. The hotel supplies movable chairs while also allowing vendors to sell clothes, records, and other goods.

3.18

In 2005 the San Francisco-based art and design collective REBAR initiated PARK(ing) Day as a way to protest the lack of green open space in the city. Participants "rent" out a metered curbside parking space for the two-hour meter limit to create a small park. Courtesy REBAR

3.19

PARK(ing) Day events have quickly spread around the country and the globe. In 2009, 700 installations were performed in 21 countries and 140 cities.
© Jeremy Shaw

PARKING LOT PICKER'S SONG

One of the characteristics of bluegrass music, besides its acoustic use of the mandolin, banjo, and fiddle, is spontaneous jam sessions associated with its nonprofessional players, known as "pickers." Bluegrass music particularly flourishes in the summertime during the numerous outdoor festivals characterized by potlucks, jam sessions, and social gatherings. The fans typically bring their instruments, and spend as much time exchanging songs and playing together as they do watching the headline acts. "Back porch pickers," many of whom have never played together, spontaneously meet not only in the parking lots of bluegrass festivals but at many other occasions as well. From local parking lot gatherings to neighborhood meetings, the phenomenon has become so popular that the term "parking lot pickers" is now synonymous with bluegrass and folk music.[23]

ACTIVISM

It is no surprise that parking lots and the cars they service raise strong feelings and opinions about their use, importance, and impact on our society. For some, they are the ultimate symbol of a car-based culture that is destroying our world. For others, they provide a vital apparatus, crucial for maintaining economic viability. Regardless of which view one concurs with, the space used for parking, whether occupied or not, provides a perfect stage for articulation of any view. Like streets and civic plazas, parking lots are spaces that allow for commentary and expression.

PARK(ING) DAY

One of the most visible displays of parking commentary and political expression comes from the efforts by the San Francisco-based art and design collective REBAR and their annual PARK(ing) Day event. The event started in 2005 as a way to protest the lack of green areas in parts of the city where a majority of the open space is dedicated to the movement and storage of private vehicles. Participants "rent" out a metered curbside parking space for the two-hour meter limit to create a small park. Feeding the parking meter enables the activists to lease precious urban real estate on a short-term basis.

PARK(ing) Day events have quickly spread around the country, and around the globe. In 2009, 700 installations were performed in 21 countries and 140 cities.[24] As the event continues to operate, participants continue to rent parking spaces to present a brief, alternative reality of curb parking while showing others the potential uses of such spaces. Through the years, this potential has evolved, adapted, and expanded to include interventions and experiments beyond the original "tree-bench-sod" park constructed by REBAR. In recent years, participants have used metered parking spaces to plant temporary urban farms, build art installations, open free bike repair shops, and extend the sidewalk's square footage through street furniture (Walklet).[25]

While PARK(ing) Day focuses on curb parking as an ideal activism medium, REBAR's notion of art and design through activism could easily be expanded to address and transform parking lots. Indeed, in their PARK(ing) Day Manifesto REBAR writes:

> Park(ing) Day is typical of the medium in which Rebar works: "niche spaces" are undervalued, or valued inappropriately for the range of potential activities within them. We believe that such niches— once identified—can be opened up to re-evaluation through creative acts. Park(ing) Day identifies the metered parking space as just such a niche within the urban landscape, and redefines it as a fertile terrain for creative, social, political and artistic experimentation. It was only through the replication of this tactic and its adoption by others that a new kind of urban space was measurably produced. . . . By providing a new venue for any kind of unmet need, re-valued parking spaces became instrumental in redefining "necessity." Thus the creative act literally "takes" place—that is, it claims a new physical and cultural territory for the social and artistic realm.[26]

TEMPORARY TRAVEL OFFICE

Parking Public is a project by the Temporary Travel Office, a group that calls itself a "quasi-fictional tourist agency." The main aim of the group is to "produce a variety of services relating to tourism and technology aimed at exploring the non-rational connections existing between public and private spaces." The group produces guides, as well as research documents and proposals for rethinking open spaces. The group has also focused on the use of parking lots. Since 2005, it has led tours of surface parking lots in cities from Hollywood to Brooklyn, and has produced a video titled *Parking Public: A Tour into the Storage of Utopia*.[27] By examining the specific histories of particular parking lots, the project seeks to generate insights into how parking "relates to the more general ideology of utopian capitalism," and "fits into our desires and frustrations for livable spaces." The following is an example of some of the background material and observational notes prepared by the group for their tour of Chicago:

- History: on September 13, 1951, the largest parking industry association, the National Parking Association, was launched at Chicago's Bismarck Hotel.
- Chicago is also home base to the second-largest parking corporation in North America, Standard Parking, Inc. (The largest is Central Parking Corporation of Nashville, Tennessee.)
- Fringe lots: Chicago was a frontrunner in the development of the 1960s surface parking lots that surrounded central business districts. Chicago's Monroe Street facility (the current site of Grant Park) was deemed one of the "most successful" in the country, with 3,000 spaces.
- Parking lots as places of protest: "Chicago Indian Village," summer 1970. Established in a parking lot at 3716 North Seminary Avenue as a response to the eviction of a Menominee woman and her children, the encampment was eventually occupied by 60 people, who were demanding better housing and educational opportunities for Chicago's Native American population.
- Parking scams: where a guy, posing as a parking lot attendant, collects the "parking fee" from an unsuspecting parker, who often finds that his/her car has been towed when he/she returns.
- The lot at 3641 North Clark Street is used as an outdoor ice skating rink in the winter.[28]

REMEDIATION

Design and planning projects like Fresh Kills Landfill in New York City and Downsview Park in Toronto attempt to explore the potential for remediation of ecological systems within urban-scarred sites. Using an array of cleanup techniques from complicated soil washing to engineered containment, these kinds of projects also offer an opportunity to test unconventional strategies, including not only the use of new materials but also the types of uses appropriate for contaminated sites. For example, sites can be regenerated and remediated through the construction of parking areas that integrate natural and absorbent elements to filter contamination. Changing the use of a contaminated site into parking is less restrictive than for other uses such as playgrounds. The lot itself could, for example, incorporate phytoremediation techniques. This approach utilizes the ability of certain plants to remove contamination from soil and water. For instance, tests have shown that certain plant species such as *Brassica juncea* (Indian mustard plant) can remove lead from contaminated sites. Other tests focus on the use of the genus *Populus*, which includes trees such as willows, poplars, and aspens, in degrading TCE (trichloroethylene, an industrial solvent).[29]

Thus parking lots can be conceptualized and designed as part of an ever-changing cycle of use and function. The lot's surface could be planned to respond to changes in environmental or use conditions. Lots that are infrequently used, such as those adjacent to large sports stadiums, could be designed with amenable vegetated surfaces to reduce environmental impacts. Others, located in flood zones, could not only act as temporary detention facilities for floodwaters but could also in the long run develop into active wetlands. These strategies have the potential for a more complete integration of parking lots not only to the city's transportation systems but also to its environmental ones.

GREEN LAWS

On January 1, 2011, CALGreen (California Green Building Standards Code Title 24, Part 11) became one of the nation's first statewide energy-efficient and environmentally conscientious set of enforceable regulations. Although the code is primarily geared toward architectural construction, it also attempts to addresses site development issues that include parking. For example, the code stipulates the allocation of parking spaces for eco-electric cars and bicycles as part of the parking lot. However, there is little consideration of specific design solutions, and few suggestions beyond a general encouragement to use permeable surfaces.

3.20

Parking lots can be conceptualized and designed as part of an ever-changing cycle of use and function. The lot's surface can be planned to respond to changes in environmental or use conditions, as does this natural low-impact lot on an archaeologically sensitive site in Caesarea, Israel. © Eran Ben-Joseph

Environmental "green" laws such as CALGreen could also integrate low-impact development themes such as reducing parking surface area, increasing trees and vegetation, and improving storm-water management. More importantly, if change is to happen, the mechanism by which these codes will be implemented should rely more on enticement and incentives rather than solely on enforcement. An example could be taken from the points award system that has been successfully used to implement the Leadership in Energy and Environmental Design (LEED) standards for green buildings and for Neighborhood Development (LEED-ND). Both LEED systems are certification programs administered by the U.S. Green Building Council (USGBC), a nonprofit organization funded largely by the building trades. According to the Natural Resources Defense Council (NRDC): "LEED certification, which includes a rigorous third-party commissioning process, offers compelling proof to you, your clients, your peers and the public at large that you've achieved your environmental goals and your building is performing as designed. Getting certified allows you to take advantage of a growing number of state and local government incentives, and can help boost press interest in your project."[30]

One of the appealing features of the LEED systems in general, and one that has in no small part contributed to their success, has been the publicity certification awards give to projects that adhere to its points systems (Certified, Silver, Gold, and Platinum). As stated by USGBC under the section "Why Certify?":

> While LEED Rating Systems can be useful just as tools for building professionals, there are many reasons why LEED project certification can be an asset:
> · Be recognized for your commitment to environmental issues in your community, your organization (including stockholders), and your industry;
> · Receive third party validation of achievement;
> · Qualify for a growing array of state and local government initiatives;
> · Receive marketing exposure through USGBC Web site, Greenbuild conference, case studies, and media announcements.[31]

As of October 2010, 7,360 commercial projects totaling one billion square feet (93,000,000 square meters) of space had received LEED certification.[32] A similar reward system applied to other features in our environment, including parking lots, would probably have a similar outcome. Just as innovative design could serve as a testing ground for emerging ideas that could later be codified, so could innovative laws influence design outcomes.

STADIUMS AND CONCERT HALLS

Stadium parking is probably the most wasteful and underutilized type of lot. Typically these large paved areas, heavily used during concerts and sport events, stand empty most of the year. For example, many football stadiums are used only during weekends in the short season. Some facilities, such as Sun Life Stadium, home of the Miami Dolphins, are addressing this issue by reducing the amount of impervious surface in the lots. The Sun Life lots' surfaces are a combination of asphalt and grass. Parking stalls are surfaced with grass (grass porous paving) and a specially designed mesh with the load-bearing capacity to support vehicles, while heavily used driving and backup lanes are asphalted. Since the parking areas are seldom occupied, their grass surface receives enough sunlight to flourish and to reduce the lots' environmental impacts. Reliant Stadium in Houston, Texas, takes another approach: rather than integrating grass porous paving stalls into all of its lots, it has a seven-acre overflow parking area that is totally surfaced with grass porous pavement.

The Zénith Concert Hall in Limoges, France, offers another intriguing planning approach to the parking lot. Designed by architect Bernard Tschumi and landscape architect Michel Desvignes, it

3.21

Electric car charging stalls, Palo Alto, California. Green Laws and Leadership in Energy and Environmental Design (LEED) standards encourage the incorporation of energy-efficient elements into parking lot design.
© Eran Ben-Joseph

3.22

A wind turbine at Great River Energy Cooperative parking lot in Maple Grove, Minnesota, generates 10 percent of the adjacent building's electricity needs.
© Dan Hendricks

3.23

Low-use parking lots at the Sun Life Stadium in Miami, Florida are perfect for pervious load-bearing surfaces that allow grass to grow. They perform the functions of asphalt pavement while reducing the environmental impacts and improving the aesthetics. © Adam First

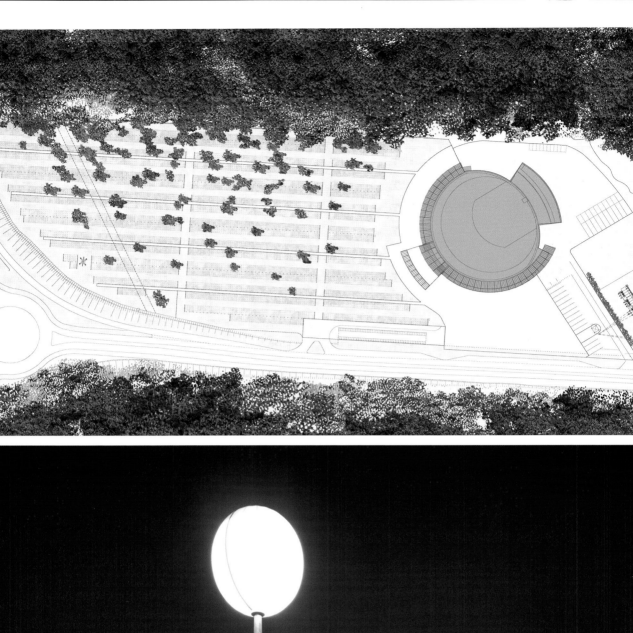

incorporates elements of the rural site into its layout and materials. Situated in a forest, the building and landscape materials reflect their immediate surroundings. Designed to be visually eye-catching both in daylight and at night, the structure curves and opens up onto the surrounding landscape through a double envelope, consisting of an outer translucent and an inner wooded surface.

Wishing to integrate the building with its surroundings while providing 1,500 parking spaces was a major challenge for the designers. Their solution was the creation of a ten-acre field covered with grass and local volcanic gravel for load-bearing capacity. Planted with 300 trees and illuminated with a combination of bollards with lights and artistic illuminating balloons, the meadow-like parking lot is not only part of the arrival and departure experience during concert times, but also an integral part of the larger landscape when not in use.

GARDENS

In his book *U.S. Landscape Ordinances* (1998), Buck Abbey provides an overview of various landscape codes and regulations as practiced around the country. These include regulations dealing with the design of areas such as street landscaping, open space planting, land use buffers, tree preservation, and parking lot screening and interior planting. A common feature of these regulations is their focus on coding individual elements while neglecting to address broader systems and contextual issues. These codes favor idiosyncratic rules and the application of generic dimensional standards such as lot configurations and specific planting requirements in a quest for uniformity. Abbey, who maintains a Green Laws Clearinghouse, acknowledges the deficiencies of existing codes and has suggested various amendments to them.[33] In a recent publication dealing with landscape codes for parking lots, he writes: "Green parking is a concept not well understood in the United States at this time, even though great ideas to form the concept are available." The definition he suggests is one that acknowledges the multiple facets of such a space and their intricate interactions. "Green Parking," he writes, "means parking areas that do environmental work, parking areas that incorporate energy efficiency, water conservation, waste minimization, pollution prevention and the use and recycling of resources, efficient materials and outdoor environmental quality in respect to air, water, soils and visual quality."[34]

By assimilating an integrated approach that avoids designing for a singular function, a new platform for design awareness can be introduced, one that accepts parking lots as productive "landscapes"—or even as gardens—that can provide ecological, social, and economic benefits.

3.24

Designed by architect Bernard Tschumi and landscape architect Michel Desvignes, the Zénith Concert Hall in Limoges, France, incorporates elements of the rural site into its layout and materials. While providing 1,500 parking spaces, the ten-acre field is covered with grass and local volcanic gravel for load-bearing capacity. Planted with 300 trees and illuminated with a combination of bollard lights and 5 luminous balloons, the parking lot is turned into a meadow-like setting. Courtesy Bernard Tschumi Architects

ORCHARD

Most municipal landscape ordinances for parking lots stipulate tree planting based on a ratio related to the lot's square footage or number of stalls. Some jurisdictions, like Sacramento and Davis, California, require that a percentage of the total paved area be shaded within a specified number of years as a requirement for the issuance of development permits. However, with little guidance on the species of trees or the actual layout for canopy coverage, some developers have clustered trees in islands or along the lot's perimeter, often resulting in large areas of unshaded pavement.[35] One way to overcome these deficiencies is to use the parking lot layout as a guide for tree planting patterns. With their existing stall and driveway configurations, almost all parking lots can easily be overlaid with an orchard plot. Planting between rows of cars as well as in islands between stalls can provide a grove-like coverage. Such a system does not interfere with parking procedures and involves a minimal loss of parking spaces.

To achieve good tree coverage, whether in an orchard-like pattern or in natural groves, parking lot regulations need to incorporate performance-based standards. Performance-based standards do not specify how things must be on the ground, but rather what they must or must not do, or what their capacity or impact should be. This type of standard was first used to control industrial activity, for which rules of permissible noise levels, smoke emissions, etc., were specified.

An example of parking lot landscaping performance standards can be seen in the West Hollywood, California, Municipal Code. Integrating a points system, the regulation requires a minimum number of canopy trees and a total number of points determined by the number of parking spaces. Other features, such as choice of paving materials, preservation of existing vegetation, and integration of pedestrian amenities, earn points toward approval.[36]

Other types of performance standards deal specifically with parking lot shading and can include policy statements such as: "Fifty percent of paved parking lots surface shall be shaded by tree canopies within fifteen years of planting." These may indicate specific methods by which the performance will be evaluated, such as: "To simplify the process of determining compliance, the true angle of deflection of natural sunlight shall not be considered. Shaded areas shall be assumed to be only those portions of a paved parking lot directly beneath the shading canopy or drip line."[37]

BLUEWATER

Bluewater is the second-largest shopping mall in the United Kingdom. Located at a former chalk quarry in Kent, England, it occupies 240 acres (97 hectares), with over 1.5 million square feet (150,000 square meters) of mixed-use space. Designed by CivicArts / Eric R. Kuhne and Associates (Eric Kuhne is the architect who won the Columbus Carscape competition mentioned in part 1), the project approach was to reclaim a large percentage of the landscape that had been lost to mining. Bluewater's triangular plan is anchored at each corner by a department store, and each of these was given a pale stone façade that echoes the surrounding chalk geology.

While the overall parking lot placement follows the traditional mall-type layout, with lots encircling the center, it is in the treatment of the lots and the approach roads that the difference can be seen. The siting of the roads takes advantage of existing quarry topography to frame vistas of the chalk cliffs, the naturalistic lakes, and the main mall building sites. The adjoining parking lots are designed as part of formal gardens with ponds, flowerbeds, and orchards, and are planted with over 4,700 trees and hundreds of thousands of aquatic plants. The parking lots and surrounding open space are connected by bike paths and walkways that allow visitors to engage in shopping, entertainment, and outdoor activities. The result is a parking landscape, where the lawns, lakes, and foliage are carefully meshed with the required acres of tarmac to accommodate cars.

SANCTUARY

All good parking lot design should incorporate and preserve existing trees. While this idea seems reasonable, few municipalities regulate preservation of existing trees. If put into place, ordinances could include a list of stipulations such as: no unlawful removal of any tree without a permit; no removal of a tree over a certain caliper dimension; special consideration for plants of significant rarity, beauty, historic background, landmark character, or cultural value; protection practices during site construction; and replacement of trees that die due to damage or disease caused during construction.

SOLAR FOREST

Many alternative energy companies have found a niche in the solar world by building shaded parking areas with solar panels fixed to the roofs of the structures. But parking lot layouts seldom take solar orientation into account, thus creating an issue with solar panel orientation. Envision Solar, a San Diego company, is developing a new mechanical device to solve this problem. Appropriately titled "solar tree," it consist of solar panels mounted on a gimbal that can track both east to west and north to south, and thus produce about 20 percent more electricity than a fixed panel.

REDUCE AND PRODUCE

The urban heat island effect can have significant implications for local climates, and parking lots are a major cause of the phenomenon. New technologies, however, may have the potential to reduce this effect. A study by the Urban Heat Island Group, part of the Lawrence Berkeley Laboratory, compared newly developed reflective asphalt with regular blacktop. On a sunny day, the reflective surface was found to be 35 degrees cooler than the standard blacktop.[38] In addition to benefiting the lot and the local climate, these cooling strategies can reduce maintenance costs for the owners of parking lots, because high temperatures are known to accelerate the processes of wear and tear to the surfacing material.

Researchers at the Worcester Polytechnic Institute have taken a different approach to the heat island effect; rather than trying to minimize asphalt's capacity to absorb heat, they are developing methods to take advantage of it.. Their idea is to draw heat out of the asphalt and harness it as useable energy. A preliminary prototype involved running water through copper pipes embedded several centimeters below the surface of the asphalt. The heated water could hypothetically be used for powering a generator or other machinery.[39]

3.25

Tustin, California. Some cities in California have developed complex shading requirement calculations to ensure proper coverage and to reach stated goals of 50 percent shading of the parking lot surface within 15 years. This has resulted in a decrease of environmental impacts and an increase in visually pleasing lots.
© Ann Forsyth

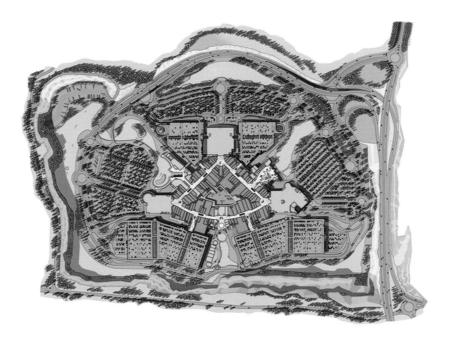

3.26

Designed by CivicArts / Eric R. Kuhne and Associates,
Bluewater is the second-largest shopping mall in
the United Kingdom, located at a former chalk quarry
in Kent. The design integrates the surrounding features
of wetlands and the chalk quarry into the parking
lot layouts. © CivicArts / Eric R Kuhne & Associates

3.27

Planted with over 4,700 trees and hundreds of
thousands of aquatic plants, the parking lots and
surrounding open space are connected by bike
paths and walkways, allowing visitors to engage in
shopping, entertainment, and outdoor activities.
© CivicArts / Eric R Kuhne & Associates

Using parking lots to improve, treat, and conserve one of our most precious resources—water—can be easily achieved. Considering that during a typical one-inch storm event more than 27,000 gallons of water (more than 102,000 liters) are washed away from a one-acre paved parking lot, techniques to capture or recharge this supply back to the aquifer are vital. As we saw in part 2, with the growing awareness of environmental impacts associated with parking lots, many cities and towns have begun to establish stormwater and flood control regulations. Unfortunately, methods used to adhere to these regulations often utilize engineered infrastructure such as concrete channels, culverts, and pipes that are aimed at quickly removing rainfall from the lot.

To better mitigate and conserve stormwater flow while complying with regulations, a simple principle can be followed: control stormwater by infiltrating it where it falls. The backbone of this stormwater paradigm change is the shift from rigid formulas to a holistic approach. At its heart is an infrastructure metamorphosis, one that changes the way we deal with the flow of water, and involves a consideration of overall stream health and water quality. Conveyance systems, which typically have comprised curbs, gutters, inlet and outlet structures, and piping systems that transport water from source areas to centralized control areas, have been reformulated. Instead, infiltration systems and nonstructural conveyors that mimic natural hydrologic cycles can be used, and parking lots provide an excellent opportunity to integrate and test these techniques.

DE-PIPING TECHNIQUES

In recent years, changes in stormwater management design have evolved as communities recognize the environmental benefits associated with less intrusive systems. Below is a short description of common techniques used to introduce an ecologically sensitive stormwater management design.

- Vegetated swales are open drainage ways designed to channel and hold runoff for short periods of time during storm events. They are intended to supplement or replace traditional pipe networks that convey runoff to a storage area for later release. The vegetation acts to filter and treat pollutants and sediment in the runoff, as well as to encourage evaporation and infiltration.

- Naturalized basins and dry ponds are large vegetated depressions that capture and detain runoff during storms. Like vegetated swales, native plants address stormwater quality by filtering runoff before infiltration. The basins are designed to hold water only during storm events, and are otherwise dry.

- Bio-retention areas and rain gardens are similar to naturalized basins in that they are also vegetated depressions designed to capture and store runoff during storm events. However, they tend to be smaller (accommodating smaller drainage areas and smaller storm events) and more deliberately landscaped, often incorporated into parking lots, cul-de-sacs, or residential gardens.

- Wet ponds are designed to permanently retain water and store runoff during and after storms. Like naturalized basins, vegetation on the pond floor acts to treat runoff and remove pollutants.[40]

Ecologically sensitive stormwater management has the potential to add value beyond the required hydrological function. Rainwater systems are not viewed merely as water disposal systems but can also be a community asset—aesthetically pleasing, integrated with art, and providing an opportunity to educate people about the working of the natural environment.

3.28

Biloxi, Mississippi. All good parking lot design
should incorporate and preserve existing
trees on its site. While this idea seems reasonable,
few municipalities regulate preservation of
existing trees. © Eran Ben-Joseph

3.29

Parking lots offer an ideal place to generate clean
energy through alternative technologies. Solar
panels such as those installed in the Sierra Nevada
Brewery in Chico, California, generate power while
also shading the lot. © Thomas Oles

ARTFUL WATER

In *Artful Rainwater Design in the Urban Landscape*, Stuart Echols argues for a paradigm change in the design approach to stormwater management. Although he endorses recent nonstructural techniques such as vegetated swales, infiltration trenches, and rain gardens, Echols also suggests that these designs need to incorporate nonhydrological features if they are to be widely used. "Non-point source pollution, water balance, and small-storm hydrology," he writes, "can be used to create projects resulting in greater user satisfaction and perceived value."[41] Parking lots, with their high impact on stormwater runoff, yet flexibility in layout design, can be used to create places integrated with "artful rainwater design" that can be both beautiful and meaningful. From integrating lush flowering gardens to artfully designed plaza-like surfaces, these stormwater approaches can transform parking lots into uniquely designed places that function as hydrological-ecological systems while also being attractive.

DESIGN ATTENTION

In the last few decades, decisions regarding the planning and design of parking lots have often been made by people who have very little understanding of design and its impacts. Planning professionals have generally been reluctant to recognize the physical design potential associated with parking lots, largely because of an ideological commitment to traffic engineering studies and trip generation formulas. This focus has resulted in the marginalization of design as an instrument to improve the lot, and a reliance on standards and codes as the instrument of shaping place, without questioning either the standards or their outcomes. In their paper "Quantity versus Quality in Off-Street Parking Requirements," Vinit Mukhija and Donald Shoup argue that planners should worry less about the quantity of parking, and pay more attention to its quality: "Planners cannot significantly improve the design of cities without reforming local parking requirements to emphasize quality over quantity. While developers may object because better design will have a higher development cost, cities can mitigate these costs by reducing or removing minimum parking requirements. Reducing parking alone will improve urban design. As a famous architect once put it, less is more."[42]

DESIGN INCENTIVES

Enforcing codes and regulations that impose a particular design solution may not always be the best way to achieve desirable results. An alternative is to incentivize and promote change through encouraging voluntary initiatives rather than through rules. As suggested in this book, parking lots provide a blank canvas that can accommodate many changes and uses within the built environment. We must not forget this aspect of these unique spaces, or all parking lots will look and function alike, and be deprived of their potential ability to be spontaneously changed. Public officials, developers, and operators of parking lots should realize that mixing uses in parking could be profitable. For example, allowing food trucks into a parking lot to create "lunch in the square" generates revenue to those vendors, to the city through permit fees, and to other local businesses (noncompeting) through increased foot traffic caused by the event.

Developers can also realize that parking lots are just as important to their development image and attractiveness as are glamorous lobbies or fancy façades. Developers of condominiums do not shy away from adding exercise and recreation facilities to lure people into buying a unit. Most understand that investment in common spaces can have positive economic outcomes. The developer, as one of the sole deciders of how a city is ultimately shaped, needs to believe that improving the parking facilities can be beneficial to both buyers and lessees of their buildings, as well as to the long-term viability of the surrounding area.[43]

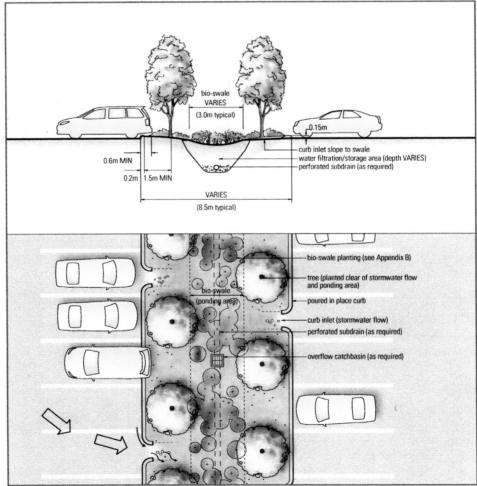

bio-swale
VARIES
(3.0m typical)

0.15m

curb inlet slope to swale
water filtration/storage area (depth VARIES)
perforated subdrain (as required)

0.6m MIN

0.2m | 1.5m MIN

VARIES
(8.5m typical)

bio-swale planting (see Appendix B)

tree (planted clear of stormwater flow and ponding area)

poured in place curb

curb inlet (stormwater flow)

perforated subdrain (as required)

overflow catchbasin (as required)

bio-swale
(ponding area)

Changes to the use and configuration of parking lots may be limited by existing zoning regulations. Yet zoning is only a vessel, a tool—yes, in many cases it is rigid within its rules, but it can also be open to change. REBAR's experience with PARK(ing) Day shows that if an activity is popularly received, public officials often find a way to make the situation work and be legally acceptable. In San Francisco, the city decided to accept PARK(ing) Day by allowing for legal construction of small pedestrian areas within curbed parking. The Pavement to Parks program, introduced in 2010 and similar to PARK(ing) Day, temporarily reclaims curb-parking areas and turns them into temporary public plazas and parks. After applying for a permit, applicants are allowed to construct a short-term project. Each installation "is intended to be a public laboratory where the City can work with the community to test the potential of the selected location to be permanently reclaimed as public open space. Materials and design interventions are meant to be temporary and easily moveable should design changes be desired during the trial run. Seating, landscaping, and treatment of the asphalt will be common features of all projects."[44]

LINGOTTO

A third of a mile long and built entirely from concrete, Fiat's Lingotto factory in Turin, Italy, was an icon of early modernism. By the early 1980s, the factory was functionally obsolete, and Fiat invited a number of prominent architects to propose ideas for its adaptive reuse. The obvious challenge presented by the Lingotto project was its sheer size (at its peak, the 2.7-million-square-foot factory complex employed 12,000 people). In addition, there was the problem of how to integrate the massive industrial complex with the surrounding urban fabric.

The winning scheme, by architect Renzo Piano, proposed complementary means of integrating building and landscape. The architects brought the building into the landscape, by copying its structural grid onto the horizontal plane and using it as an organizing element for the placement of trees. Conversely, they brought the landscape into the building, by importing lush greenery to the previously barren inner courtyards.

Whereas many of the other architects had proposed tearing down large sections of the original building, Piano's scheme leaves it largely intact. Instead, it adopts a clever strategy of blurring the lines between the building, its surrounding infrastructure (parking lots), and the larger landscape. In an early description of his design concept, Piano described a "mineral" system for work and a "vegetal" system for leisure: "The unifying and connecting feature of the whole scheme will be nature. Nature reconquers the spaces left vacant by industry and railways, thus healing the wounds inflicted between the area and its surroundings."[45] Piano saw the parking lots around the buildings as an opportunity to connect the massive architecture to the more refined fabric of the city. He eliminated all regular parking islands and curbs, and planted rows of trees in a dense grid. The result is a checkerbox of tree trunks guiding parked cars and pedestrians, all under a soft canopy of foliage. What one sees in Lingotto's parking lots design is a carefully choreographed version of the fabled image of nature reclaiming the postindustrial landscape.

3.30

Duck, North Carolina. Designed with a pervious surface and with an acceptance of occasional minor flooding, parking lots can provide an excellent opportunity to hold stormwater runoff and recharge the aquifer. © Eran Ben-Joseph

3.31

Ecologically sensitive stormwater management techniques such as bio-filtration medians have the potential to add value beyond the required hydrological function. Such systems would not be viewed merely as water disposal systems but also as attractive habitat environments within the lot. Courtesy City of Toronto

3.32
Lodi, Italy. Ecological approaches can transform
parking lots into attractively designed places that
assist natural hydrological systems. © Thomas Oles

3.33
When redesigning the old Fiat Lingotto factory in Turin,
Italy, architect Renzo Piano was faced with the
challenge of integrating the massive building into its
surroundings. His solution was to turn the paved
surfaces around the factory into parking lot gardens.
By eliminating all regular parking islands and curbs,
and planting rows of trees in a dense grid, Piano
created a checkerbox of tree trunks guiding parked
cars and pedestrians, all under a soft canopy of foliage.
© Brian Pugh

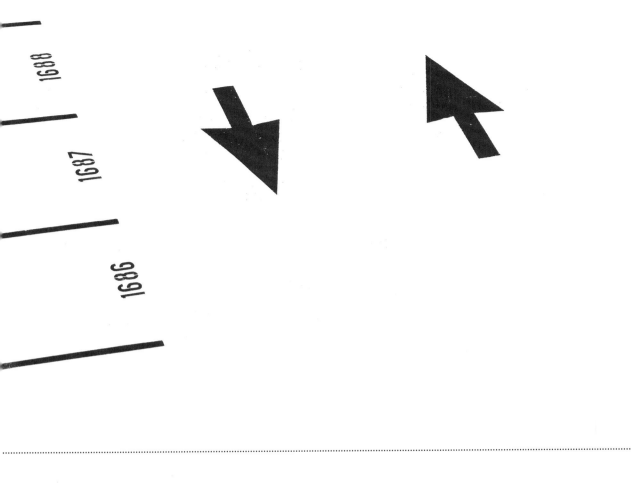

MUSING A LOT

In 1950, Walt Disney released "Motor Mania," a short cartoon featuring Goofy as the split personality "Mr. Walker" and "Mr. Wheeler." The cartoon opens with Mr. Walker as a jovial, good-natured pedestrian walking down the street to his parked car, and stopping along the way to smell flowers and greet his neighbors. When he reaches his car and sits behind the wheel, however, he undergoes a transformation, suddenly becoming a rude, belligerent, and borderline violent driver. As the cartoon narrator explains:

> The average man is a creature of strange and unorthodox habits. Take the case of Mr. Walker. Mr. Walker lives in a quiet, respectable neighborhood; he is a typical, average man. Considered a good citizen, and of average intelligence. He is a kindly man, courteous, punctual and honest. Mr. Walker wouldn't hurt a fly. Nor step on an ant. He believes in live and let live. Mr. Walker owns a motorcar and considers himself a good driver. But, once behind the wheel, a strange phenomenon takes place. Mr. Walker is charged with an overwhelming sense of power. His whole personality changes, abruptly he becomes an uncontrollable monster—a demon driver. Mr. Walker is now Mr. Wheeler—a motorer [sic].[1]

Something similar to this "split personality" is at play in our attitudes toward parking lots; we demand convenient parking everywhere we go, and then learn not to see the vast, unsightly spaces that result. For many, parking lots are a necessary evil—we hate them, but we can't do without them.

4.1
Haile Village Center and parking lot area,
Gainesville, Florida. © Facelessb

Indeed, the surface parking lot has ravaged large swaths of the landscape; it (along with the highway) was a key element in the destruction of the small-scale pedestrian urban fabric associated with "good" cities. The American historian Lewis Mumford warned in 1964: "The right to have access to every building in the city by private motorcar in an age when everyone possesses such a vehicle is actually the right to destroy the city."[2] The architect and urban planner Andres Duany adds sarcastically:

> Actually, there is a point at which a city can satisfy its parking needs. This situation can be found in many small, older American cities and is almost always the result of the same history: at mid-century, with automobile ownership on the rise, a charming old downtown with a wonderful pedestrian realm finds itself in need of more parking spaces. It tears down a few historic buildings and replaces them with surface parking lots, making the downtown both easier to park in and less pleasant to walk through. As more people drive, it tears down a few more buildings, with the same result. Eventually, what remains of the old downtown becomes unpleasant enough to undermine the desire to visit, and the demand for parking is easily satisfied by the supply. This phenomenon could be called the Pensacola Parking Syndrome, in honor of one of its victims.[3]

While there may be good reasons to associate our desire for owning, driving, and parking a car with the problems of the contemporary city, the reality is that we could have done a better job designing for it. The car did not destroy the city, the poorly designed spaces for it did. Roads could have been designed to be more than just conduits for vehicles, and parking lots could have been more than just repositories for stationary vehicles.

As the examples in this book illustrate, a successful parking lot is one that integrates its site conditions and context, takes measures to mitigate its impacts on the environment, and gives consideration to aesthetics as well as the driver-parker experience. Designed with conscientious intent, parking lots could actually become significant public spaces, contributing as much to their communities as great boulevards, parks, or plazas. For this to happen, we need to release ourselves from the singular, auto-centric outlook for the use of the lot. We need to reevaluate conventional parking requirements against evolving lifestyles and changing priorities. Above all, we need to accept that parking lots are primary settings for many aspects of public life for Americans, and for a growing number of others across the globe. For something that occupies such a vast amount of land, and is used on a daily basis, the parking lot has received scant attention. It's time to ask: what can a parking lot be? It's time to rethink the lot.

4.2
Molding everyday places like parking lots through simple,
generative interventions can transform the way we
live and interact with our surroundings. Our intent should
neither be to champion the abolition of the surface
parking lot nor to advocate the creation of strict codes
that dictate its design, but rather to recognize that
parking lots could be some of our great public spaces.
© dpa / Corbis

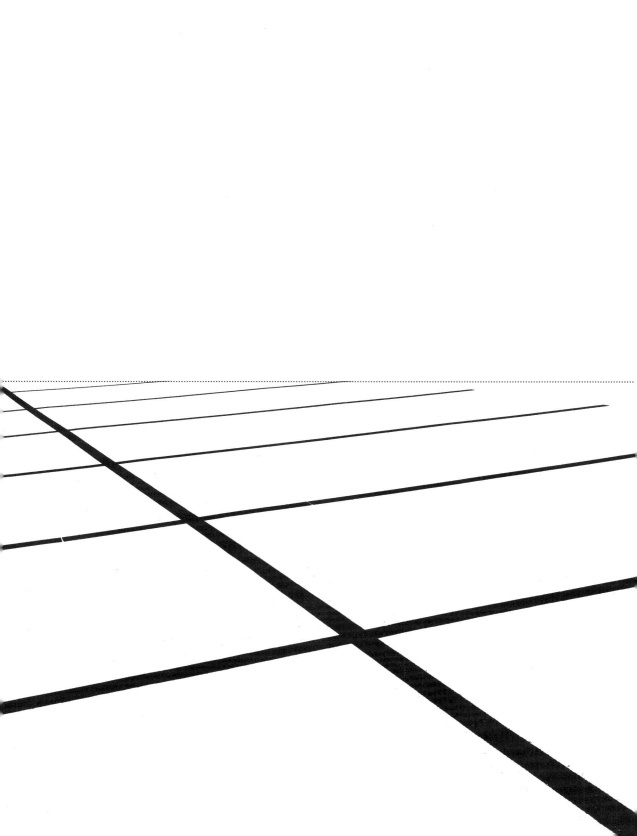

NOTES

A LOT ON MY MIND

1. For a full discussion of the estimated numbers of surface parking spaces in the United States, see part 1, "Occupied" section. Estimates are based on Mikhail Chester, Arpad Horvath, and Samer Madanat, "Parking Infrastructure: Energy, Emissions, and Automobile Life-Cycle Environmental Accounting," *Environmental Research Letters* 5, no. 3 (2010).

2. According to the U.S. Census (2005), the average commuting time to work is 100 hours a year, or about 30 minutes per working day. A study done at the University of California, "Activities Contributing to Total Energy Expenditure in the United States: Results from the NHAPS Study," *International Journal of Behavioral Nutrition and Physical Activity* 1, no. 4 (2004), estimates that American drive an average of 100 minutes a day. On the basis of these findings, one can roughly estimate that on average personal cars are used for about an hour and a half in a 24-hour period, or 4–7 percent of the time, and are parked the rest of the day. See also Donald Shoup, *The High Cost of Free Parking* (Chicago: University of Chicago Press for American Planning Association, 2005), 624–625.

1 A LOT IN COMMON

1. Paul Groth, "Parking Gardens," in Francis Mark and Randolph Hester, eds., *The Meaning of Gardens* (Cambridge, MA: MIT Press, 1990), 130.

2. John Brinckerhoff Jackson, *Landscape in Sight: Looking at America* (New Haven: Yale University Press, 1997), 76.

3. See, for example, Edward Relph, *Place and Placelessness* (London: Pion, 1976); Yi-Fu Tuan, *Space and Place: The Perspective of Experience* (Minneapolis: University of Minnesota Press, 1977); James Howard Kunstler, *The Geography of Nowhere: The Rise and Decline of America's Man-Made Landscape* (New York: Touchstone, 1993); Marc Augé, *Non-places: Introduction to an Anthropology of Supermodernity* (London: Verso, 1995).

4. Quoted in Mary Lou Gallagher, "A Parking Sketchbook—New Solution to Old Problem," *Planning* (October 1991), 12.

5. American Society of Landscape Architects, 2005 General Design Award of Honor, 12,000 Factory Workers Meet Ecology in the Parking Lot, Canton, GA, Michael Van Valkenburgh Associates, Inc., New York, NY, Professional Awards Jury Comments, <http://www.asla.org/awards/2005/05winners/172.html> (accessed March 17, 2009).

6. Catherine Miller, *Carscape: A Parking Handbook* (Columbus, IN: Washington Street Press, 1988), 28.

7. Ibid., 1.

8. Ibid., 40.

9. Frederick Steiner and Kent Butler, eds., *Wiley Graphic Standards, Student Edition*: *Planning and Urban Design Standards* (Hoboken, NJ: American Planning Association, John Wiley, 2007), 166.

10. Ibid.

11. For a detailed description of the historical development of parking through zoning, see part 2.

12. Donald Shoup, "Truth in Transportation Planning," Transportation Research Board 80th Annual Conference, 2001, Washington, DC.

13. David Bergman, *Off Street Parking Requirements*, American Planning Association, Planning Advisory Service Report #432 (Chicago: American Planning Association, 1991).

14. U.S. Environmental Protection Agency, *Our Built and Natural Environments: Technical Review of the Interaction between Land Use, Transportation, Environmental Quality* (Washington, DC: EPA, 2001), 50.

15. Shoup, "Truth in Transportation Planning," 2.

16. Cambridge, Massachusetts, "Zoning Ordinance. Article 6.10. Intent and Applicability of Parking and Loading Requirements," <http://www2.cambridgema.gov/cdd/cp/zng/zord/zo_article6_1335.pdf > (retrieved March 15, 2010).

17. See for example Paul Jacques Grillo, *Form, Function, and Design* (New York: Dover, 1975).

18. Brian O'Looney and Neal Payton, "Seeking Urbane Parking Solutions," *Places* 18, no. 1 (2006), 40–45.

19. Leonard Hopper, *Landscape Architecture Graphic Standards* (New York: Wiley, 2007), 256.

20. Amélie Y. Davis, Bryan C. Pijanowski, Kimberly D. Robinson, and Paul B. Kidwell, "Estimating Parking Lot Footprints in the Upper Great Lakes Region of the USA," *Landscape and Urban Planning* 96, no. 2 (May 2010), 30, 68–77.

21. Victoria Transport Policy Institute, "Transportation Cost and Benefit Analysis: Techniques, Estimates and Implications" (2009), <http://www.vtpi.org/tca/tca0504.pdf>, pp. 5.4–8 (retrieved March 16, 2010).

22. Mikhail Chester, Arpad Horvath, and Samer Madanat, "Parking Infrastructure: Energy, Emissions, and Automobile Life-Cycle Environmental Accounting," *Environmental Research Letters* 5, no. 3 (2010).

23. Christopher Alexander, Sara Ishikawa, Murray Silverstein, with Max Jacobson, Ingrid Fiksdahl-King, and Shlomo Angel, *A Pattern Language* (New York: Oxford University Press, 1977), 505.

24. U.S. Census Bureau, "United States, Selected Economic Characteristics," *American Community Survey* (2009), <http://factfinder.census.gov/servlet/STTable?_bm=y&-geo_id=01000US&-qr_name=ACS_2009_1YR_G00_S0802&-ds_name=ACS_2009_1YR_G00_&-_lang=en&-redoLog=false&-format=&-CONTEXT=st> (retrieved December 26, 2010).

25. Katharine Mieszkowski, "We Paved Paradise," <http://www.salon.com/news/feature/2007/10/01/parking/print.html> (retrieved May 16, 2010); Bryan Pijanowski, "Parking Spaces Outnumber Drivers 3-to-1, Drive Pollution and Warming" (2007), Purdue University, <www.purdue.edu/unsx/2007b/070911PijanowskiParking.html> (retrieved March 13, 2010).

26. Richard Cassady and John E. Kobza, "A Probabilistic Approach to Evaluate Strategies for Selecting a Parking Space Source," *Transportation Science* 32, no. 1 (January 1998), 30–42.

27. Victoria Transport Policy Institute, "Transportation Cost and Benefit Analysis: Techniques, Estimates and Implications," 5.4–15; also Northwestern University, "Community Invited to Discuss Evanston Parking Plans," *NewsCenter* (2006), <http://www.northwestern.edu/newscenter/stories/2006/01/parking.html> (retrieved April 16, 2009).

28. Victoria Transport Policy Institute, "Transportation Cost and Benefit Analysis: Techniques, Estimates and Implications," 5.4–15.

29. Ibid., 5.4–10.

30. U.S. Environmental Protection Agency, *Parking Spaces / Community Places: Finding the Balance through Smart Growth Solutions*, 231-K-06-001 (Washington, DC: EPA, 2006), 9.

31. Ibid., 9–10.

32. H.R. 1216, 110th Congress, 2007, Cameron Gulbransen Kids Transportation Safety Act of 2007, also called "K.T. Safety Act of 2007," <http://www.govtrack.us/congress/bill.xpd?bill=h110-1216> (retrieved December 10, 2010).

33. "Pedestrian Accidents Involving Children: Facts, Figures & Statistics" (2008), <http://www.articlesbase.com/law-articles/pedestrian-accidents-involving-children-facts-figures-statistcs-701769.html> (retrieved September 15, 2010).

34. Joshua Prince and Macky Pamintuan (illustrator), *I Saw an Ant in a Parking Lot* (New York: Sterling Publishing 2007), 5.

35. Ibid., 8.

36. Ibid., 17.

37. Ibid., 21.

38. Tom Sturges, *Parking Lot Rules & 75 Other Ideas for Raising Amazing Children* (New York: Ballantine Books, 2008), 3.

39. Ibid., 3–4.

40. Trae, *In the Hood ft Yung Joc* (video, 2006), <http://www.youtube.com/watch?v=SJ1NKcqiibl> (retrieved February 2, 2010).

41. Ibid.

42. Kathleen Ziegenfuss, "Constructing Use in Surface Parking Lots: Strategies for Enhancing Lots as Part-time Public Spaces," Master of City Planning thesis (Massachusetts Institute of Technology, 2009), 108.

43. Tailgating.com home page, <http://www.tailgating.com/index.html> (retrieved January 15, 2011).

44. Bob Kimbell, "Tailgating King Joe Cahn Finds Recipe for Football Happiness," *USA Today*, October 23, 2010, <http://content.usatoday.com/communities/gameon/post/2010/10/tailgating-king-joe-cahn-finds-recipe-for-football-happiness/1> (retrieved January 11, 2011).

45. Alyssa Martuch, "Protocol for Pre-Gaming," *Ferris State Torch*, September 30, 2009, <http://www.fsutorch.com/2009/09/30/arts-entertainment/protocol-for-pre-gaming/ >(retrieved January 11, 2011).

46. "Tailgating: The History," *American Heritage Magazine* 56, no. 5 (October 2005), <http://www.american-heritage.com/articles/magazine/ah/2005/5/2005_5_11.shtml> (retrieved January 11, 2011).

47. M. L. Lyke, "Wal-Mart Campers Like Parking Lots' Low Prices," *Seattle Post-Intelligencer Reporter*, July 23, 2002, <http://www.seattlepi.com/local/79628_walmart23.shtml?dpfrom=thead> (retrieved January 11, 2011).

48. Andrew Cornwall, "The Economic Effects in Nova Scotia of the RV Overnight Parking Ban and Aspects of Campground Minimum Standards," Nova Scotia, 2006.

49. American Rivers, Natural Resources Defense Council, and Smart Growth America, *Paving Our Way to Water Shortages: How Sprawl Aggravates the Effects of Drought* (Washington, DC: Smart Growth America, 2002).

50. Eric Betz, "No Such Thing as Free Parking," *ISNS*, December 1, 2010, <http://www.insidescience.org/research/no-such-thing-as-free-parking> (retrieved February 6, 2011).

For the original study, see Chester, Horvath, and Madanat, "Parking Infrastructure."

51. Jeffrey Luvall and Dale Quattrochi, "What's Hot in Huntsville and What's Not: A NASA Thermal Remote Sensing Project," NASA Global Hydrology and Climate Center, 1996.

52. Kathleen Wolf, *Trees, Parking and Green Law: Strategies for Sustainability* (Stone Mountain, GA: Georgia Forestry Commission, Urban and Community Forestry, 2004).

53. San Francisco Planning Department, "Guide to the San Francisco Green Landscaping Ordinance—Amendments to San Francisco's Municipal Codes" (2010).

54. Wolf, *Trees, Parking and Green Law*, 27.

55. City of Portland [Oregon], Planning and Zoning Title 33, Chapter 33.248, Landscaping and Screening (2010).

56. City of Sacramento, Planning and Building Department, "Parking Lot Tree Shading Design and Maintenance Guidelines" (2003).

57. Roger Trancik, *Finding Lost Space: Theories of Urban Design* (New York: John Wiley, 1986), 4.

58. Lyn Lofland, *The Public Realm: Exploring the City's Quintessential Social Territory* (Piscataway, NJ: Transaction, 2009), xv.

59. Ziegenfuss, "Constructing Use in Surface Parking Lots," 109.

60. Berkeley Flea Market, "News: Save the Flea Market," <http://www.berkeleyfleamarket.com> (retrieved January 13, 2011).

61. Paul Newly, "Leimert Park Farmers Market," *Annenberg Digital News*, University of Southern California, February 28, 2009, <http://www.neontommy.com/2009/02/leimert-park-farmers-market> (retrieved January 17, 2011).

62. "The Principality of the Mists: Fighter Practices within the Principality," <http://mists.westkingdom.org/fighter_practices.php> (retrieved February 1, 2011); Ellen Miramontes, "Parking Lot Parks: The Parking Lot as a Multipurpose Space," Master of City Planning thesis, University of California Berkeley, 1999, 38–40.

63. David Levinson, "The Next America Revisited," *Journal of Planning Education and Research* 22 (August 2, 2003), 332.

64. Nate Hooper, "Keeping the Faith, and the Parking Spot," *Times Union* (Albany, NY), 2010, <http://www.timesunion.com/local/article/Keeping-the-faith-and-the-parking-spot-598984.php#ixzz1CcYXBMxL> (retrieved January 23, 2011).

65. "Churches: Drive-In Devotion," *Time*, November 3, 1967, <http://www.time.com/time/magazine/article/0,9171,837478,00.html> (retrieved January 23, 2011).

66. Los Angeles Conservancy, "Preservation Alerts and Issues: Self-Help Graphics & Art Building," <http://www.laconservancy.org/issues/issues_selfhelp.php4> (retrieved February 1, 2011).

67. Barry Ruback and Daniel Juieng, "Territorial Defense in Parking Lots: Retaliation against Waiting Drivers," *Journal of Applied Social Psychology* 27, no. 9 (1997), 821–834.

68. Leonard Scheff and Susan Edmiston, *The Cow in the Parking Lot: A Zen Approach to Overcoming Anger* (New York: Workman Publishing, 2010).

69. David Millward, "Is This the End of the Road for Traffic Lights?" *The Telegraph* (November 4, 2006), <http://www.telegraph.co.uk/news/uknews/1533248/Is-this-the-end-of-the-road-for-traffic-lights.html> (retrieved January 29, 2011).

70. Timothy Crowe, *Crime Prevention through Environmental Design: Applications of Architectural Design and Space Management Concepts* (Louisville: University of Louisville, National Crime Prevention Institute, 2000), 36.

71. Garnett Shaffer and L. M. Anderson, "Perceptions of the Security and Attractiveness of Urban Parking Lots," *Journal of Environmental Psychology* 5 (1983), 320.

2 LOTS OF TIME

1. Joseph Ingraham, *Modern Traffic Control* (New York: Funk and Wagnalls, 1954), 18.

2. Maxwell Lay, *Ways of the World: A History of the World's Roads and of the Vehicles That Used Them* (New Brunswick, NJ: Rutgers University Press, 1992), 325.

3. Ingraham, *Modern Traffic Control*, 18.

4. *Oxford English Online Dictionary*, <http://www.oed.com.libproxy.mit.edu/> (retrieved May 7, 2010).

5. Ibid.

6. William Lloyd, "The Parking of Automobiles," *University of Pennsylvania Law Review and American Law Register* 77, no. 3 (January 1929), 336.

7. Ruth Reichard, "Infrastructure, Separation, and Inequality: The Streets of Indianapolis Between 1890 and 1930." Master of Arts Thesis. Indiana University, Department of History, 2008.

8. Catherine Miller, *Carscape: A Parking Handbook* (Columbus, IN: Irwin-Sweeney-Miller Foundation, Washington Street Press, 1988).

9. Ibid.

10. John Howard Brown, *The Twentieth Century Biographical Dictionary of Notable Americans* (Boston: Biographical Society, 1904), vol. 8.

11. William Tindall, "The Origin of the Parking System of This City," Records of the Columbia Historical Society (Washington, DC) 4 (1901), 81.

12. Ibid., 88.

13. Robert James Forbes, *Notes on the History of Ancient Roads and Their Construction* (Amsterdam: N.V. Noord-Hollandsche Uitgeverij-MIJ, 1934).

14. Ibid.

15. Charles Singer and Eric Holmyard, *A History of Technology* (Oxford: Oxford University Press, 1958).

16. Stull Holt, *The Bureau of Public Roads: Its History, Activities and Organization* (Baltimore: Johns Hopkins University Press, 1923), 5.

17. Ira Baker, *A Treatise on Roads and Pavements* (New York: Wiley and Sons, 1918), 378; Charles Morrison, *Highway Engineering* (New York: Wiley and Sons, 1908), 170.

18. *Scottish Law Reporter*, October 1891–July 1892 (Edinburgh: John Baxter and Sons), 661.

19. "Some Advantages of the Automobile," *Horseless Age* 10, no. 15 (October 8, 1902), 377.

20. Edward Fisher, *Vehicle Traffic Law* (Evanston, IL: Northwestern University Traffic Institute, 1961), 39.

21. William Phelps Eno, "Street Traffic Legislation and Regulation in the United States of America," *Journal of Comparative Legislation and International Law*, 3rd ser., 7, no. 4 (1925), 238–247.

22. See Eno Transportation Foundation, <http://enotrans.com/index.asp?Type=B_EV&SEC={59B58976-4BBF-43AF-9CC0-14664D065FD5}> (retrieved December 2, 2010.); Charles Tilden, "New York's First Printed Traffic Regulations Issued Just 25 Years Ago," *American City*, November 1928, 135; William Phelps Eno, "The Storage of Dead Vehicles on Roadways," in *The Automobile: Its Province and Its Problems*, Annals of the American Academy of Political and Social Science 116 (November 1924), 169–174.

23. Eno, "Street Traffic Legislation and Regulation in the United States."

24. Ibid.

25. Highway Transport Committee of the U.S. Council of National Defense, "Suggested General Highway Traffic Regulations," *American City* 21, no. 4 (1919), 355.

26. Eno, "The Storage of Dead Vehicles on Roadways."

27. Ibid., 170.

28. Ibid., 170–173.

29. Hawley Simpson, "Downtown Storage Garages," in Planning for City Traffic, Annals of the American Academy of Political and Social Science 133 (September 1927), 83.

30. "Blowouts Blamed on Careless Parking," Science News-Letter 34, no. 11 (September 10, 1938), 173.

31. Eno, "The Storage of Dead Vehicles on Roadways," 172.

32. Austin MacDonald, "Parking Facilities Outside the Traffic Zone," in *Planning for City Traffic*, 78.

33. Wilbur S. Smith and Charles S. Le Craw, *Parking* (Saugatuck, CT: Eno Foundation for Highway Traffic Control, 1946), 68.

34. Ibid., 69.

35. Virginia Scharff, "Of Parking Spaces and Women's Places: The Los Angeles Parking Ban of 1920," *NWSA Journal* 1, no. 1 (1988), 39.

36. Ibid., 43.

37. Ibid., 39.

38. Ibid., 45.

39. Ibid., 46.

40. MacDonald, "Parking Facilities Outside the Traffic Zone," 79.

41. Davis Jackson, "Parking Needs in the Development of Shopping Centers," *Traffic Quarterly*, January 1951, 32.

42. Ibid., 33–34.

43. Ingraham, *Modern Traffic Control*, 226.

44. John Jakle and Keith A. Sculle, *Lots of Parking: Land Use in a Car Culture* (Charlottesville: University of Virginia Press, 2004), 10.

45. Charles Le Craw and Wilbur Smith, "Zoning Applied to Parking," *Traffic Quarterly* 1, no. 1 (January 1947), 11.

46. Ibid., 28.

47. YiLing L. Chen-Josephson, "No Place to Park: The Uneasy Relationship between a City and Its Cars," *Yale Law School: Student Prize Papers* (2007), paper 22, 9.

48. Ibid., 11.

49. Stroud vs. City of Aspen, 1975. 532 P.2d 720, <http://scholar.google.com/scholar_case?case=67727333 46198163015&q=Stroud+v.+City+of+Aspen,++(1975).&hl=en&as_sdt=2,22&as_vis=1> (retrieved February 13, 2011).

50. "Off-Street Parking," *Society for Science and the Public Newsletter* 49, no. 9 (March 2, 1946), 139.

51. Le Craw and Smith, "Zoning Applied to Parking," 11.

52. Edward G. Mogren, *Parking Authorities* (Saugatuck, CT: Eno Foundation, 1953), 14.

53. Simone Baribeau, "Miami Looks at City's Parking Revenue to Fund Reserves, Make Bond Payments," *Bloomberg—Business and Financial News*, August 2, 2010, <http://www.bloomberg.com/news/2010-08-02/ miami-looks-to-parking-revenue-to-meet-bond-payments-replenish-reserves.html> (retrieved February 18, 2011).

54. Harold Lewis and Earl Morrow, "Layout and Design of Parking Lots: Aesthetic Considerations," *Traffic Quarterly*, January 1952, 27–39.

55. Ibid., 29.

56. Ibid., 30.

57. Ibid., 32–34.

58. Theodore Matson and Wilbur Smith, *Traffic Engineering* (New York: McGraw-Hill, 1955), 3.

59. Institute of Traffic Engineers, *Traffic Engineering Handbook* (Washington, DC: Institute of Traffic Engineers, 1965), 478.

60. American Automobile Association, *Parking Manual* (Washington, DC: American Automobile Association, Traffic Engineering and Safety Department, 1946), foreword.

61. Ibid., 108.

62. *Parking Design Manual* (Parking and Highway Improvement Contractors Association, Education Fund, 1968), 2.

63. Parking Standards Design Associates, *A Parking Standards Report* (Van Nuys, Sherman Oaks, CA: Parking Standards Design Associates, 1971), preface.

64. Urban Land Institute, *The Community Builder Handbook* (Washington, DC: Urban Land Institute, 1954), 171–172.

65. Ibid., 177.

66. Ibid.

67. Urban Land Institute and International Council of Shopping Centers, *Parking Requirements for Shopping Centers: Summary Recommendations and Research Study Report* (Washington, DC: Urban Land Institute, 1999).

68. Edmund R. Ricker, *Traffic Design of Parking Garages* (Saugatuck, CT: Eno Foundation for Highway Traffic Control, 1948).

69. Parking Standards Design Associates, *A Parking Standards Report*, 1.

70. Ibid., 2.

71. Robert H. Burrage, *Parking* (Saugatuck, CT: Eno Foundation for Highway Traffic Control, 1957), 137.

72. Roy Rosenzweig and Elizabeth Blackmar, *The Park and the People: A History of Central Park* (Ithaca, NY: Cornell University Press, 1992), 481–498.

73. Christopher Gray, "Favored by Sheep and Other Celebs," *New York Times*, January 13, 2011, <http://www.nytimes.com/2011/01/16/realestate/16streetscapes.html?ref=tavernonthegreen> (retrieved May 15, 2011).

74. One example of a different approach can be seen in the parking lot design for the Miles Laboratory in Elkhart, Indiana, in 1971. Based on integrated landscape elements, the parking lot was designed with extensive landscaping, gaps in curbs to allow for water drainage into the median strips, and large vegetated depressions to allow for water infiltration. These features are common in today's approach to green engineering and Low Impact Development, but were unique in the 1970s. For more information on the Miles Laboratory parking lot, see Gary Robinette, *Parking Lot Landscape Development* (Reston, VA: Environmental Design Press, 1976).

75. Robinette, *Parking Lot Landscape Development*, 103.

76. Ibid., 107.

77. Victor Gruen, "Save Urbia for the New Urbanites," *AIA Journal*, February 1960, 36.

78. Philip Rothschild, "The Clean Air Act and Indirect Source Review: 1970–1991," *UCLA Journal of Environmental Law and Policy* 10 (1992), 337.

79. An earlier porous parking prototype was constructed in 1973 at the University of Delaware in Newark. In 2000, after 27 years, the parking lot was sealed. Records show that during that period no special maintenance was required except the use of less deicing salt during the winter months. See Bruce Ferguson, *Porous Pavements* (CRC Press, 2005), 466.

80. Robert Cervero, *Transit-Oriented Development in the United States: Experiences, Challenges, and Prospects* (Washington, DC: Transportation Research Board, 2004), 187.

81. Anton Troianovski, "New York City Is Most Expensive Place to Park a Car in the U.S.," *Wall Street Journal*, February 20, 2011, <http://blogs.wsj.com/metropolis/2010/07/15/americas-most-expensive-place-to-park-manhattan/> (retrieved February 20, 2011).

82. Cervero, *Transit-Oriented Development in the United States*, 187.

83. Ian McHarg, "The Place of Nature in the City of Man," in *Urban Revival: Goals and Standards, Annals of the American Academy of Political and Social Science* 352 (March 1964), 1–12.

3 LOTS OF EXCELLENCE

1. "Dia Art Foundation—Dia," <http://www.diacenter.org/contents/page/info/102> (retrieved March 8, 2011).

2. Mark Stevens, "Soho on the Hudson," *New York Times Magazine*, 2003, <http://nymag.com/nymetro/arts/art/reviews/n_8705/> (retrieved March 7, 2011).

3. Architect Lyn Rice, personal interview, March 7, 2011.

4. National Recreation and Park Association, *A Primer on the Techniques of Parking Vehicles at Public Recreation Facilities* (Wheeling, WV: Vollmer Associates, 1965), 5.

5. *Hengistbury Head Management Plan* (Bournemouth Borough Council, January 2011).

6. City of Cambridge, Arts Council, "Performance in Black and White: Toshihiro Katayama," November 30, 2004, <http://www2.cambridgema.gov/CAC/Exhibitions/Material_Choice_Case_Studies_Katayama.cfm?minor> (retrieved March 8, 2011).

7. Ibid.

8. Kevin Lynch, Tridib Banerjee, and Michael Southworth, *City Sense and City Design: Writings and Projects of Kevin Lynch* (Cambridge, MA: MIT Press, 1996), 397–398.

9. Colin Buchanan, ed., *Traffic in Towns: A Study of the Long Term Problems of Traffic in Urban Areas* (London: Ministry of Transport, Her Majesty's Stationery Office, 1963).

10. Niek De Boer, *Woonwijken: Nederlandse Stedebouw* 1945–1985 (Rotterdam: Uitgeverij 010, 1987); Niek De Boer and Ina Klaasen, *De Stad van Niek De Boer: Polemische Beschouwingen over Stad en Regio* (Delft: Publikatieburo Bouwkunde TUDelft, 2005).

11. Eran Ben-Joseph, "Changing the Suburban Street Scene: Adapting of the Shared Street (Woonerf) Concept to the Suburban Environment," *Journal of the American Planning Association* 61, no. 4 (1995).

12. *Shared Space: Ruimte voor iedereen* (Fryslân Province, Leeuwarden, The Netherlands, 2005), 45; available at <www.shared-space.org>.

13. "A Parking Lot Can Mean a Lot to Kids," *Nation's Business* 58 (April 1, 1970), 4.

14. Michael Southworth and Eran Ben-Joseph, *Streets and the Shaping of Towns and Cities* (Washington, DC: Island Press, 2003), 145.

15. Cited in Alexandra Schwartz, *Ed Ruscha's Los Angeles* (Cambridge, MA: MIT Press, 2010), 133.

16. Montague's classification system has been presented as a Web site: <www.strayshoppingcart.com>; a book: *The Stray Shopping Carts of Eastern North America: A Guide to Field Identification*, published in 2006; and an installation with shows in 2002, 2004, and 2006.

17. James Wines, *De-Architecture* (New York: Rizzoli International, 1987), 110.

18. By 2000, the art installation was in disarray and partially destroyed. When local attempts to renovate and preserve it were unsuccessful, the line of 15 asphalt-covered cars was demolished and removed from the shopping center in 2003.

19. SITE, *Architecture as Art* (New York: St. Martin's Press, 1980), 28.

20. Fred Kaplan, "Shakespeare and Company," *Boston Globe*, City Edition, July 23, 1998, A3.

21. Ibid.

22. Kathleen Ziegenfuss, "Constructing Use in Surface Parking Lots: Strategies for Enhancing Lots as Part-time Public Spaces," Master of City Planning thesis (Massachusetts Institute of Technology, 2009).

23. The popularity of the term can be seen in the fact that at least six songbooks with the title *Parking Lot Picker* are available for sale to musicians. See for example Bruce Dix, *Parking Lot Picker's Songbook Bass Edition* (Mel Bay Pub, 2010).

24. "Park(ing) Day 2010 |About PARK(ing) Day," <http://parkingday.org> (retrieved March 5, 2011).

25. See <http://walklet.org> (retrieved March 4, 2011).

26. PARK(ing) Day Network, "Resources," <http://my.parkingday.org/page/resources-1> (retrieved March 5, 2011).

27. Temporary Travel Office, "Parking Public," <http://temporarytraveloffice.net/hollywood/parking.html >(retrieved March 5, 2011).

28. Temporary Travel Office, "Parking Public: Parking in Chicago's Wrigleyville" (2010), <http://temporarytraveloffice.net/hollywood/ChicagoZineWeb.pdf> (retrieved March 4, 2011).

29. Leonard Hopper, *Landscape Architectural Graphic Standards* (Hoboken, NJ: Wiley, 2007), 802.

30. "NRDC: Building Green—LEED Certification Information," *NRDC: Natural Resources Defense Council— The Earth's Best Defense*, <http://www.nrdc.org/buildinggreen/leed.asp> (retrieved March 6, 2011).

31. U.S. Green Building Council, *LEED for New Construction and Major Renovations Rating System Version 2.2* (Washington, DC: U.S. Green Building Council, 2005), 4.

32. U.S. Green Building Council, "About LEED" (2010), <http://www.usgbc.org/DisplayPage. aspx?CMSPageID=1720> (retrieved March 6, 2011).

33. See <http://www.greenlaws.lsu.edu/>.

34. Buck Abbey, "Ordinance: Sustainable Parking Landscape Design," *Landscape Architect and Specifier News* 27, no. 2 (February 2011), 26.

35. See part 1, "Landscape" section, and part 2, "City Ordinances" section.

36. West Hollywood Municipal Code, Title 19, Chapter, 19.28.100, "Surface Parking Area Standards."

37. Fresno, California, Planning and Development Department, *Performance Standards for Parking Lot Shading* (2006).

38. See <http://retailtrafficmag.com/mag/retail_turning_heat_heat/> (retrieved March 3, 2011).

39. See <http://www.alternative-energy-news.info/solar-energy-asphalt-roads/> (retrieved March 3, 2011).

40. Definitions based on "Managing Stormwater: Best Management Practices," Perkiomen Watershed Conservancy, Schwenksville, PA, <http://www.greenworks.tv/stormwater/index.htm> (retrieved March 9, 2011).

41. Stuart Echols, "Artful Rainwater Design in the Urban Landscape," *Journal of Green Building* 2, no. 4 (2007), 1.

42. Vinit Mukhija and Donald Shoup, "Quantity versus Quality in Off-Street Parking Requirements," *Journal of the American Planning Association* 72, no. 3 (2006), 307.

43. Some of these ideas have been developed through the work of Kathleen Ziegenfuss's MCP thesis. See Ziegenfuss, "Constructing Use in Surface Parking Lots."

44. See San Francisco Planning Department, "Pavement to Parks," <http://sfpavementtoparks.sfplanning.org> (retrieved March 8, 2011).

45. "Renzo Piano Progetto Lingotto, Torino," *Domus* 675 (September 1986), 38.

MUSING A LOT

1. "Motor Mania" can be watched online: "YouTube—Goofy in 'Motor Mania' (1950)," <http://www.youtube.com/watch?v=mZAZ_xu0DCg> (retrieved March 10, 2011).

2. Lewis Mumford, *The Highway and the City* (New York: New American Library, 1964), 23.

3. Andres Duany, Elizabeth Plater-Zyberk, and Jeff Speck, *Suburban Nation: The Rise of Sprawl and the Decline of the American Dream* (New York: North Point, 2000), 162.

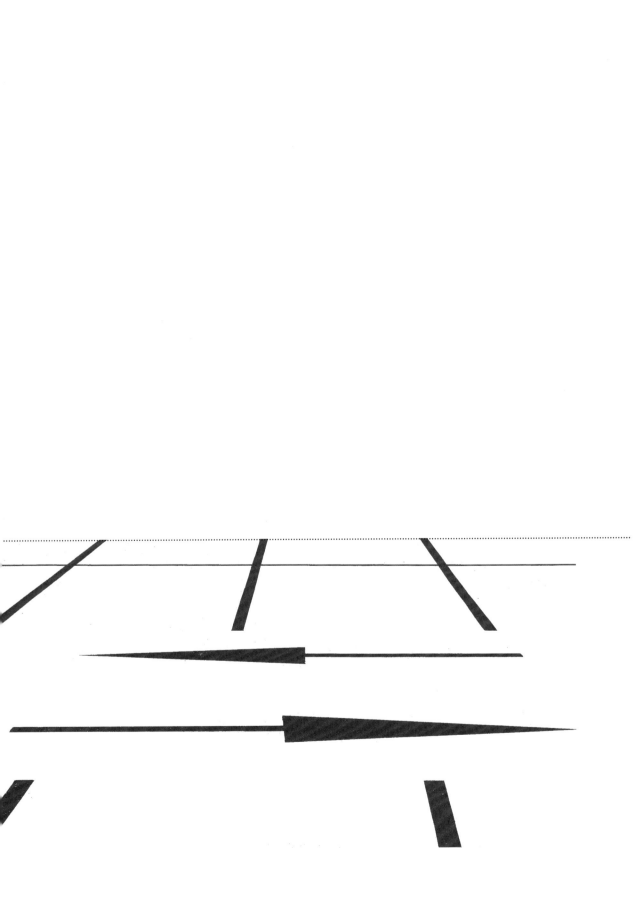

OTHER REFERENCES

Aitken, Thomas. *Road Making and Maintenance*. London: Charles Griffin and Company, 1907.

Alexander, Christopher. *A New Theory of Urban Design*. New York: Oxford University Press, 1987.

Barter, Paul. "Off-Street Parking Policy without Parking Requirements: A Need for Market Fostering and Regulation." *Transport Reviews* 30, no. 5 (2010).

Berger, Alan. *Drosscape: Wasting Land in Urban America*. New York: Princeton Architectural Press, 2006.

Burow, Elizabeth. "Play Ground." Thesis, master of architecture, Massachusetts Institute of Technology, 2005.

Childs, Mark C. *Parking Spaces: A Design, Implementation, and Use Manual for Architects, Planners, and Engineers*. New York: McGraw-Hill, 1999.

City of Toronto. *Design Guidelines for "Greening" Surface Parking Lots*. Toronto: City Planning Department, 2007.

Corwin, Margaret A. *Parking Lot Landscaping*. Chicago: American Society of Planning Officials, 1978.

Crawford, Margaret, John Chase, and John Kaliski. *Everyday Urbanism*. New York: Monacelli Press, 1999.

Davidson, Michael, and Fay Dolnick. *Parking Standards*. Chicago: American Planning Association, Planning Advisory Service, 2002.

Dimensions of Parking. 2010. Washington, DC: Urban Land Institute.

Duany, Andres, Jeff Speck, and Mike Lydon. *The Smart Growth Manual*. New York: McGraw-Hill, 2010.

Ferguson, Erik. "Zoning for Parking as Policy Process: A Historical Review." *Transport Reviews* 24, no. 2 (2004).

Henley, Simon, and Sue Barr. *The Architecture of Parking*. New York: Thames & Hudson, 2007.

Hill, Jim, Glynn Rhodes, Steve Vollar, and Chris Whapples. *Car Park Designers' Handbook*. London: Thomas Telford, 2005.

Huber, Jeff. *Low Impact Development: A Design Manual for Urban Areas*. Fayetteville, AR: University of Arkansas Community Design Center, 2010.

Jackson, John Brinckerhoff. In *Landscape in Sight: Looking at America*. Ed. Helen Lefkowitz Horowitz. New Haven: Yale University Press, 1997.

Jakle, John A., and Keith A. Sculle. *Lots of Parking: Land Use in a Car Culture*. Charlottesville: University of Virginia Press, 2005.

Jenks, Dennis A. *Parking Publications for Planners*. Chicago: Council of Planning Librarians, 1993.

Kay, Jane Holtz. *Asphalt Nation: How the Automobile Took Over America, and How We Can Take It Back*. Berkeley: University of California Press, 1998.

Kemp, Roger. *Cities and Cars: A Handbook of Best Practices*. Jefferson, NC: McFarland & Co, 2007.

Kraft, Walter H., Wolfgang S. Homburger, and James L. Pline. *Traffic Engineering Handbook*. Washington, DC: Institute of Transportation Engineers, 2010.

Litman, Todd. *Parking Management Best Practices*. Chicago: American Planning Association, 2006.

Longstreth, Richard W. *The Drive-In, the Supermarket, and the Transformation of Commercial Space in Los Angeles, 1914–1941*. Cambridge, MA: MIT Press, 1999.

Lynch, Kevin. *Site Planning*. Cambridge, MA: MIT Press, 1971.

Mayer, Madelaine Rose. "Parking Lots: An Investigation of Public Space in the Contemporary American City." Thesis, master of science in architecture, Georgia Institute of Technology, 2005.

McCluskey, Jim. *Parking: A Handbook of Environmental Design*. London: E. & F. N. Spon, 1987.

McDonald, Shannon Sanders. *The Parking Garage: Design and Evolution of a Modern Urban Form*. Washington, DC: Urban Land Institute, 2007.

McShane, Clay, and Joel A. Tarr. *The Horse in the City: Living Machines in the Nineteenth Century*. Baltimore: Johns Hopkins University Press, 2007.

Meijerink, Paula. *On Asphalt*. Cambridge, MA: Harvard Graduate School of Design, 2009.

Morgan, Micah. "Park Space." Thesis, master of architecture, Rice University, 2005.

Parking: Selected References, 2008. 2008. Washington, DC: Urban Land Institute.

Spaces, Parking, and Community Places. *Finding the Balance through Smart Growth Solutions*. Washington, DC: United States Environmental Protection Agency, 2006.

Parr, Martin. *Parking Spaces*. London: Chris Boot Books, 2007.

Robinette, Gary. *Parking Lot Landscape Development*. Reston, VA: Environmental Design Press, 1976.

San Mateo County. *Sustainable Green Streets and Parking Lots Design Guidebook*. San Mateo County, CA: Water Pollution Prevention Program, 2009.

Shoup, Donald C. *The High Cost of Free Parking*. Chicago: University of Chicago Press for American Planning Association, 2005.

Smith, Mary S. *Shared Parking*. Washington, DC: Urban Land Institute, 2005.

Southworth, Michael, and Eran Ben-Joseph. *Streets and the Shaping of Towns and Cities*. Washington, DC: Island Press, 2003.

Spirn, Anne Whiston. *The Granite Garden: Urban Nature and Human Design*. New York: Basic Books, 1984.

Stilgoe, John R. *Outside Lies Magic: Regaining History and Awareness in Everyday Places*. New York: Walker, 1998.

Venturi, Robert, Denise Scott Brown, and Steven Izenour. *Learning from Las Vegas*. Cambridge, MA: MIT Press, 1977.

OTHER REFERENCES

INDEX

Redwood City, California, 107
regulations, xi, xx, 8, 9, 11, 13, 37–38, 55, 57,
    62–67, 72, 76, 82, 90–91, 93–95, 120, 123–
    124, 129–130. *See also* requirements;
    standards; zoning
religious rituals, 43–45
remediation, 118–119
requirements, xvi, 8, 21, 76, 101, 108, 109, 129
    environmental, 93, 123
    formula (ratios), 16, 89, 91
    historical, 76, 95
    law, 76, 79
resorts, 48, 49, 101
revenues, 29, 81, 90, 129
reverse-angle parking, 94, 95
Ricker, Edmund R., 89
risk, 107. *See also* danger
Roads and Bridges Act (UK), 61
Rockville, Maryland, xiv
Roman roads, 58, 59
Rome, 53, 55, 59
runoff. *See* stormwater
Ruscha, Ed, 109, 110

safety, 8, 24, 47, 60, 63, 91, 107
San Francisco, California, 28, 69, 116, 117, 131
    Green Landscaping Ordinance, 37
sanitation, 8, 60, 62
Schwartz, Martha, 112, 113
screening, 7, 9, 37, 80, 103, 123
Sculle, Keith A., xvii
sculptures, 7, 111
Seaside, Florida, 108, 109
seating, 131
Sennacherib, 53
shade, xvi, 37, 38, 83, 91, 124, 125
Shakespeare in the Parking Lot, 114, 115
shared parking, 106, 107, 108
shared space, 106–107
shared streets. *See* shared space
shopping carts, 110
shopping malls, 4, 16, 30, 45, 82, 101, 105, 124
Shoup, Donald, xvii, 8, 129
shrines, 44, 45
sidewalks, 9, 39, 57, 59, 107, 117
Sierra Nevada Brewery (Chico, California), 128
SITE (Sculpture in the Environment), 110–112
Smart Growth America, 32
social behavior, 4, 45
Solana Office Complex (Westlake, Texas), 101
solar power, 125, 128
Somerville, Massachusetts, 27, 38–39, 114, 115
Southern California Mobile Food Vendors
    Association, 27

spaces (parking)
    costs of constructing, 17
    total area consumed, 14, 18
    total number, 8, 9
    per vehicle, 8, 16
speed, 32, 60, 62, 63, 106, 107
spontaneous activities, xix, 3, 39, 105, 113, 129
stadiums, 12, 28, 119, 120, 121
standards, 7–9, 16, 24, 69, 76, 83–91, 107–109,
    120–124, 130. *See also* regulations
statistics, 45
storm drainage. *See* stormwater
stormwater, 18, 32, 33, 127, 131
    bio-retention, 127
    code, 91, 93, 120
    detention ponds, 33
    innovation, 4, 95, 96, 127, 129
    swales, 127, 129
    technique, 37, 127
Stray Shopping Cart Project, 110
streams, 32
streets, 61, 79, 84
    health, 62
    historical, 53, 55, 57, 59
    redesign, 47, 105, 106, 107
suburbs, 12, 43, 53, 73, 81, 105, 111, 113
Sun Life Stadium (Miami, Florida), 120, 121
supermarkets. *See* malls
swales. *See* stormwater
Syracuse, New York, 94, 95

tailgating, xix, 25, 28
Technology Transfer Program (EPA), 95
teenagers, 25, 26
Temple, Texas, 90
Temporary Travel Office, 118
Thirtyfour Parking Lots, 109
Tokyo, Japan, xvi
Toronto, Canada, 118
Trae, 25
traffic, 55, 66, 69, 81, 84, 105–106
    calming, 107
    regulations, 47, 62, 63, 67
Traffic Engineering Handbook, 84
Trancik, Roger, 39
transect, 9
transportation engineering, 84
trees, 4, 7, 19, 33, 37, 83, 91
    preservation of existing, 125
trellises, 7
Tresaguet, Pierre-Marie-Jérôme, 59
trip generation formulas, 8, 11, 129
Tschumi, Bernard, 120, 123
Tulsa, Oklahoma, 14